# Connections

## How a Network of Energies Magically Connects Us All

BOB BRICKLEY

LONG STORY SHORT PUBLISHING COMPANY

# CONTENTS

It was easy to decide
to whom I wanted to dedicate this book.
To all the gifted people I have been honored
to meet and grow with over decades.
For their love. For their trust. For the growth
I have experienced by simply knowing them.
You have fueled my passion, my life purpose...
*Helping people grow.*
My gratitude and thanks for this truly overflows.
My "connection" with each of you has been
one of God's many blessings that have defined me...
allowed me to find my real self.

# INTRODUCTION

*"God created man because he loved stories."*

"Fireflies" That's how my mornings usually open. With "fireflies." Messages blinking before my eyes. Maybe you've experienced some of the same? Angels, spirits maybe? For years, I've wondered where these flashes come from. They're almost photographic at times. They fascinate me. "Go get that one! And that one! Put them in the jar before they disappear." When I share this with others? Others cast a skeptical eye. More don't respond at all.

The reality? These "fireflies" are connections of energy surrounding us all... trillions of microscopic lines flowing everywhere. Every second of every day. Think of trusting your "instincts"... "feeling it". Getting a "buzz." Being "in the zone." Or one of those "I was just thinking about you!" experiences. Frequencies of energy that connect with one another and create these feelings. These are examples of energy at work. Its network drives and connects us to much of life... a dimension we experience often but have little awareness of.

Think about random stuff like... Khama... six degrees of separation. Other surprising examples of happenings are inexplicable. Most times, we refer to these as coincidences. All... are the energy at work. Trillions of energy lines converging at different frequencies. Seeking other frequencies that match. When they "find" each other? All those inexplicable happenings above occur.

*In truth, the entire universe is an indivisible whole in which all things are interconnected, in which nothing exists in isolation. No one of us lives in isolation from another. We are all a product of the CONNECTIONS between us.*

My desire to share inspired this book. Distribute ideas and discoveries? Tell stories about my experiences with people I've worked with for decades. It's been a series of defining life lessons. What makes different people "tick?" Finding keys, ways to guide people along this journey called "life." A never-ending pursuit that calls out to us. Draws each of us to travel our path. Your path ... unique, like no other.

I asked a friend to review my book while it was about 70% done. "What do you think?" I asked. "I came away feeling like I just attended a number of church services." he replied. And you know, I think that's how I felt while I was writing it. Like I was somehow conducting a church service.

Over the many years I've been coaching, maybe I never fully realized it, but like any coach, I can only call the plays. I can't run them. It's up to each player on the field to do their job. Run the plays. This book offers numerous "plays" I've written for you to consider "running." While my hope is you will act on some of what's here, that is totally up to you. I make no judgment. My passion is helping you find your most effective way forward. See all the CONNECTIONS that guide you along the path you choose.

I will not attempt to coach you here. I will offer stories and experiences that may inspire you to change or better direct your own way forward. There is a reason the windshield is five times larger than the rear-view mirror. Learn from the past. Focus on the road ahead. But growth only lives on the windshield. This is where I hope this book directs you. Connects you with learnings from your past, while propelling you into a future filled with new discoveries, personal growth.

Life is a process, not an event. Be aware of takeaways you may have following each piece. See how they connect to help you see the road ahead... make your journey successful.

I've been a manager, a business builder... and today, a Life Coach. Worked with hundreds of great people. Using a lot of strategies, tactics... the things that drive businesses forward. The mechanics and structural issues are critical in delivering a positive result. I spent twenty-five years in corporate America. Leading and developing financial services firms. My primary value for them was always about delivering the bottom line.

I left the corporate world in 1997. Became a consultant to financial services businesses across the US. Similar to those I had served previously. The difference here? I'd always been the boss before. I wasn't the boss anymore. The business leaders I worked with were in charge, not me.

But I kept acting as though I was in charge. I couldn't understand why my clients didn't do what I told them to do. Learned quickly that they wanted me to help them find their own answers to their problems. Not have me tell them what to do. I learned a critical life lesson.

*People do things for their reasons... not yours.*

This is when I first discovered how "energy" comes into play. Financial services firms operate on an "invisible assembly line." There's no physical product. The product is an intangible. Firms like these are successful... because of the quality of their people, more than any other factor. The products they offer have become commodities. It's hard to distinguish one from another. Thus, the people are primarily responsible for the success of the business.

What made one practice "tick"? What was it about their "assembly line" that made their firm successful? After I'd worked with a few, I noticed a clear distinction. I'll call it "flow." The successful firms operated with a coherent, shared value system. An "energy" connection of their own. A healthy culture. Driven by trust, collaboration, and teamwork. All the pieces just seemed to fit. Never flawlessly, but effectively. Grounded by the value system they would live by, installed by the leader(s). Executed and brought to life within the business by the teammates themselves.

Oh, there were strategies and tactics that were required to grow. But the trust and focus on doing the job together as a team fueled the "flow" of how the business operated. Created the connection, the "energy" that made a difference. All were fully engaged, fully invested.

I found my role gradually moved from strategist to psychologist. I needed to address the mindsets of the team members more than the mechanics of running the business. The relationships between the leaders and their people. How they behaved. Respected one another. I helped them identify the particular "energy" frequency that best worked for them. That was my real job. Get the "energy"... the relationships right, and the business operated effectively... smoothly.

To prove my point...

Years ago, a new client of mine asked if I could meet him at 6 am for our first meeting. I arise early. "Sure... see you at 6." I Ubered to his office the next morning. As I entered the front door, the smell of coffee greeted me. The day's Wall Street Journal sat on a table. It was 5:55. And there, at the receptionist's desk, sat a young lady. *"Good morning, Mr. Brickley. Welcome!"*

Blow me over with a feather... really?! I later learned that my young welcomer had checked the office calendar the day before. Saw I was coming in. Her job? To greet all visitors to the business. She decided she would be in the office at 6. As I approached her to thank her for her kindness, I noticed a name plate sitting on her desk. Inscribed on its face...

*"Mary Stuart, Director of First Impressions".*

I met with my client at 6 am as planned. Knew in advance what I'd learn about him, his team of 26. This would be one firm I'd work with that... got it. Embraced the importance of values, culture over strategy. The value of a team connected. A team alive with healthy "energy." They enjoyed operating in the "flow" I mentioned earlier. Mary Stuart was the first of many I met that morning who made everything "flow."

I've had a book inside me for decades. Been encouraged many times to write one. One about great people... like Mary Stuart. I have an office library filled with over four hundred books. I've read most of them cover to cover. The subject matter? Personal development, leadership, human dynamics. This education drew me to a life dedicated to a simple mission...

*"Helping people grow... so they will go forth and help others grow."*

Clients have challenged me regarding my qualifications as a consultant and life coach. "Where are your credentials?" I show them a picture of my library filled with 400 books. All on personal growth, spirituality. "I'm homeschooled." After that, my qualifications have never been questioned.

The first time my vision of our invisibly connected world came to me fifty years ago during a Sunday service at St. David's Church. A small fifty-seat gem in my hometown of Philadelphia. The same church where my parents had been married twenty-nine years earlier.

As I sat in the front pew, I turned to my left. There, peering brightly through an open window, was a laser-like beam of light. A huge oak tree stood outside, its blanket of leaves swaying back and forth, tossing in a brisk wind. This mesmerized me. As the leaves passed back and forth across the light, I noticed they never blocked the light's path. What was going on? This chilled me at first. Then warmed me. Magically, at that moment, I was connected to something very different.

That thin, bright ray of light had taken me somewhere new. I believe to this day that my faith was birthed that Sunday. This was my first experience with the network of "energy" that magically connects us all. That drives much of life.

I'm sure you've had moments like this too. Think back. You've never forgotten them. Small energetic "sparkings" ... experiences that have captured you. "Fireflies." Moments like these are subtle but vivid. Easy to miss. Yet invaluable when embraced.

There was a second experience of mine that opened me to accepting this unique energy field. In 1976, I lived through illness, suffered from manic depression. Celebrated America's bicentennial in 1976 being treated in a mental hospital. Please, don't think I'm putting myself in this category. But Lincoln, Gandhi, FDR... John Kennedy. These distinguished men suffered their own forms of mental illness, too. A thought that comforted me then. Dealing with their mental challenges made these men great. Similarly, I felt dealing with my own illness lifted me to another level of awareness, capability. This experience changed me.

That day in church. My bout with mental illness. As I look back, both opened something in me that has directed my path. Connected me with a frequency of energy that sparked new life in me.

I began writing a blog five years ago. "The Space Between the Notes" has been a joyful hobby. Two hundred and fifty plus blog posts later? That book I mentioned is ready to launch.

CONNECTIONS is a compilation of posts from my blog. The theme? Some of the innumerable commonalities, connections we all share with one another. CONNECTIONS is validation that it's within our power to process, influence, even control the "energy" network surrounding us.

As I embark here, most of what follows is mine. My stories. My experiences. But I hope as you read them, you will recall your own. Those experiences you can relate to. Those that trigger memories about your own life. Today... yesterday.

You may find this book to be a bit random. That's because it is. We'll zigzag back and forth. From one thought to another. Try to see each blog post as my attempt to validate that energy "connections" abound. Resonate all around us.

The best description of what's written here connects me with Forest Gump. Remember? *"Life is like a box of chocolates. You never know what you're going to get."* So, like a box of chocolates, I offer my own box of "chocolates" with ninety-plus pieces in it. And *"You'll never know what you're going to get."*

I leave it to you to find your own favorite pieces here. Don't try to grasp a broad, overarching message. Look for the finer points in each short piece that strike you. Your own "firefly" moments might help more clearly direct your path in life. As they magically have and continue to direct mine.

### How to Read This Book ...

As I described in the introduction, this book is a collection of short writings. Teachings, concepts, and experiences I've accumulated over decades. Designed to help you learn and grow. For those of my "vintage," you will remember *"Reader's Digest"*... a collection of short pieces. Each stands on its own as a lesson or anecdote that you might find of interest.

Purposely, I've limited each piece to a page and a half or so. Short, pithy messages that have fueled my career, my life experience.

*You will find some of the book's themes repeated throughout different pieces. I hope that this will allow my messages to reach each of you in your own way.*

It's a fact that most books have something in common. Many of us will read the first ten, fifteen pages of a book and then put it down. Never to return. Thus, my posts are a page short. Brevity makes it easier for the reader to complete each one.

Freely move around from piece to piece. While all my writings have relevance to the "connections" theme of the book, each stands on its own. Some will hit you more than others. Pick the book up. Put it down. Pick it up again. I've designed the book to be accessed in this way.

Whether you complete my book or not, I hope you'll find nuggets of wisdom here.

*I believe when intelligence, instinct, and emotion combine... wisdom evolves.*

Wisdom gives you confidence there is always more to learn. That you can travel as far as you want along whatever path you choose. Allowing your network of energy to guide you magically along your journey.

## Who Am I?

*No resume here. Rather, I offer things that defined my personality, character, and value system.*

There were many key life experiences that urged me to write CONNECTIONS. I had a normal childhood. But I was born with a blind and severely crossed left eye. Made my early school years tough. You know how mean ten-year-olds can be. "Ha, ha. You're so ugly." Thought from that day forward, "I'm not good-looking." Ha! Still feel some of this... sixty plus years later.

But as I look back, this was an early challenge that drove me to achieve. Have success in life. Went to a great prep school in Philadelphia. Excelled athletically. I was a class leader. But I suffered through some loneliness as a teenager. My school was thirty minutes from home. Far away from my classmates who all got together on weekends without me. This was when I first experienced the depression that was part of the mental illness I mentioned earlier. An illness that eventually changed me paradoxically, in most ways, positively.

College followed prep school. Athletic success continued. Had few dates. Remember? I didn't think I was very attractive.

Shortly after college while working for an insurance company in Philadelphia, I had an experience that magically connected me with a deeper part of myself. Changed me forever. I was asked by my first boss to join him and thirty of his best insurance clients to play golf one day at Pine Valley Golf Club in New Jersey. Indisputably the #1 golf course in the world. I was stunned by the place. Being a golf nut, this place was my "emerald city" Nirvana! While golfing there was incredible, Pine Valley didn't change me that day. This did. All guests at the event wore suits to dinner. As I was departing through the living room of the clubhouse following dinner, my boss was sitting, talking to three of his clients. Not knowing I could hear what he was saying, he said this.

*"You see that kid leaving there? He's going to be president of something someday."*

Because of the immense respect I had for this man. I never forgot his comment. It connected with me, well, in a very spiritual way to a higher self of mine. To a future that in fact saw me lead, serve as president of businesses and organizations from that day forward. This had been a moment that has guided me.

Think back. See if you can remember an experience that might have directed the course of your life.

Eventually, I married a beautiful lady... she adorned this less attractive guy. We had two beautiful daughters.

I built businesses in Philadelphia, Hartford, Connecticut and lastly Atlanta for a large financial services company. They downsized me in 1997 after twenty years there. I was fifty-one. The loneliness, depression I'd experienced as a teenager suddenly returned and kicked back in. I had to work through a very hard transition period. Depressed. Out of a job. What could I do? I'd decided I would never return to corporate America.

Ah ha! I had a brainstorm! My success in business had always centered on team building. That was it. It had been about the people. I would help other financial service firms build their teams. My vision? *Growing your business by growing your people.* For the next ten years, I traveled the country consulting with firms. After almost two million miles on Delta, I'd had enough of flying. No more planes for me. I asked myself at age 69, "What's next?" Whatever was next? I knew it had to involve connecting people. Them with others. Me with them. Building relationships always had to be the core of my "what's next." Today I enjoy a third career as a Life Coach.

### What's my point?

Balancing successes with setbacks is essential to achieving personal growth. You must embrace it all. Knowing that each experience, good or bad, is a stepping stone. Oh, it's not easy. If it was, everybody would be doing it! I've always told myself, *"God gives us good. He gives us bad. But He never gives us wrong."*

"Connections"... unexplainable happenings. We often refer to them as coincidences. "What an amazing coincidence!" We tend to dismiss these all as random occurrences. Never considering the possibility that there is a lot more going on here that we don't fully understand. Who can say what is going on? But I suspect that occasionally, we hear a "whisper"... a "firefly" that goes something like this: "You've turned up in the right place at the right time. Consider this." Coincidental? I think not.

*I'm asked often... "Why do you write?" My philosophy? Always begin with "Why." So... here goes. Before I embark on this project. Here's... Why I write.*

## On Writing

A dear friend helped me acknowledge why I write. He sent me this. It so perfectly encapsulates why I write. I had to include it here.

*"Writing can be a true spiritual discipline. Writing can help us concentrate, to get in touch with the deeper stirrings of our hearts, to clarify our minds, to process confusing emotions, to reflect on our experiences, to give*

*artistic expression to what we are living, and to store significant events in our memories."*

*"Writing can also be good for others who might read what we write. Often, a difficult, painful, or frustrating day can be "redeemed" by writing about it. By writing, we can claim what we have lived and thus integrate it more fully into our journeys. Then writing can become lifesaving for us and sometimes for others, too."*

*"Writing. Opening a Deep Well is not just jotting down ideas. Often, we say, "I don't know what to write. I have no thoughts worth writing." But much good writing emerges from the act of writing itself. As we simply sit down in front of a sheet of paper and express in words what is on our minds or in our hearts, new ideas emerge, ideas that can surprise us and lead us to inner places we hardly knew were there. One of the most satisfying aspects of writing is that it can open in us deep wells of hidden treasures that are beautiful for us as well as for others to see."*

*Making Our Lives Available to Others. One argument we often use for not writing is this: "I have nothing original to say. Whatever I might say, someone else has already said it, and better than I will ever be able to." This, however, is not a good argument for not writing. Each human being is unique and original, and nobody has lived what we have lived. What we have lived, we have lived not just for ourselves but for others as well."*

Writing can be a creative and invigorating way to make our lives available to ourselves and to others. I must trust that our stories deserve to be told. And in the process may discover that the better I tell my stories, the better I will want to live them. This is my perspective for sure. Why I write.

# CHAPTER 1
# PREPARATION

# PREPARATION

*"Most of success in life begins
with the miracle of preparation."*

I learned long ago when solving a problem, 80% is about defining the problem; 20% is about finding the solution. The quality of the preparation determines the quality of the outcome. Think of setting the GPS before traveling... or reading the instructions before assembling that fifty-piece IKEA furniture set. Start right? You'll finish right.

Those I've coached over the years are always "antsy" when our work begins. My process is methodical. Begins with introspection. Getting the relationships right. The coachie with himself first. Then, him with me. Moving next to key relationships; especially family members. We move on to identify the issues we need to address. Behavior changes essential for personal growth. All are looking for relief from something... disentangling themselves from a problem they're facing. Resolving a personal conflict they might be struggling with. It takes courage to accept my help. I have great admiration for all who reach out to me.

When I work with business leaders, I hear this a lot. "What's all this 'psychobabble' got to do with the result? How does this affect the bottom line?" They want me to "fix" their problem... now! Can't understand why moving too quickly to achieve the result might send them off course. "What am I paying this guy for?"

I introduce them to one of the early pillars of my coaching...

The "Paradox of Speed."

*The best way to speed up. Is to slow down.*

But most I coach don't see it this way. They think the best way to speed up... is to speed up! I watch many people run through their days like drunken sailors. They think there's always time... always more time? No. Time is finite. Slowing allows you to savor important things more fully. Family, leisure, and appreciation of the gifts bestowed us. Make better decisions. When you slow? Become more aware? Watch how the slowing, taking time to make decisions puts you on a better course. So hard to do today in a world so addicted to speed. Thus my first rule as coaching begins? *We will slow down to gain speed.*

Ok... we're preparing for launch. You are about to embark on a journey that may change your life. Or at least give you an awareness of how you might change.

Before launching? An absolute necessity. It's all about preparation. The first 15% of any process ahead will determine the success of the remaining 85%. The message here? The first 15% may be the most important part of your journey. Stick with me.

# The Space
# Between the Notes

*I begin this with a description of my Blog, "The Space Between the Notes", which birthed most of what follows. So much of life is filled with activity. As Nike tells us, "Just do it!" But you'll see as you read through this book, it's the quality of our decisions that directs us along the path of the life we choose. The pauses between your actions guide you to make better choices.*

In a Frank Sinatra interview decades ago, he was asked, "Mr. Sinatra, can you tell us why your music is so dynamic, so celebrated by so many?" Sinatra replied, "It's pretty simple. I always spend more time on the pauses in my music than I do on the notes themselves." The spaces between the notes. Thus, seven years ago, I began my writing. Random topics, thousands of words later...

"The Space Between the Notes" has evolved.

I encourage you to "pause" following your reading of each short piece. Create your own puzzle pieces like thoughts. May be hard to discern how they all come together at first. But you will find they eventually form a pattern. You'll see. This process should reveal a lot about you. What makes sense? What does not? Your challenges. Your character. Your passions. All the traits and qualities that drive the actions you take.

*As we begin here, central to all the concepts and teachings offered in this book? There is one thing that I want you to grasp. First. Everything you encounter in life. Every experience. Every relationship... everything in your life... is all about YOU. Let me elaborate....*

## It all begins... with "You."

Job #1 as we begin. Connecting You with You. Sound like an odd place to start? This is a central focus of this book. The foundation of living a successful life is based on your relationship with yourself. Life begins with YOU.

Think about it. How many of us live fully authentic, confident lives? I'm not saying you're not okay with yourself. I would just ask you this, "Do you truly love yourself?" How you see yourself. It's always about You. Taking responsibility. For everything. No excuses. No complaints. No regrets. No blaming others or circumstances. Saying "No" to those activities, or commitments others ask you to engage in that take you away from really just being you. Because in the final resolve? Everything is all about you. All about Me! And the choices we make.

Think of this as a "game of tag" with yourself. You're always... IT!

I had a coach for over twenty years. Connected with him in 1997. Just after being abruptly downsized from the company I'd worked with for twenty years. It devastated me. College tuitions, mortgages... but more hurtful than anything else? My reputation and my identity were in free fall. I was a mess. All this rekindled my manic-depressive tendencies Yeah, I got a healthy dose of "Woe is me!" I found myself in the worst place to be in life— I was a victim of my circumstance. Meeting my coach was providential. He lived in California. Our time together? All over the phone. Met him for the first time five years after our work began. Chris Andersonn is an amazing person. A metaphysicist. The student of human consciousness. Learned a ton. My work with him inspired much of what I share here.

I asked Chris one day, "Coach, how am I doing so far?" "Frankly, Bob.,' he answered. "You're kind of a pain in the ass." Oh great, I thought. I'm paying this dude for this. But you know? He was right. I'd had a hard time grasping what he was teaching me. The reality that everything in life, every frustration, every misfortune, every experience... good or bad. Had nothing to do with anyone, any condition or circumstance... it was all about Me.

Everything in my life was solely my responsibility. Hard to understand, I know. It took me a long time to see what Chris was teaching me. It's always about "You." Taking responsibility is the adult choice. Trust building with yourself is essential if one is to personally grow.

Think about this. I have an issue bothering me. Why didn't I get that promotion? That consulting engagement didn't go well. Ugh! So many things just seemed to "happen" to me. "Woe is me." No... what had I done to make these things happen?

I once had a toxic relationship with a good friend. My coach asked me, "Tell me, Bob. What's the problem here?" Boy, did he get a bucket full... "He only talks about himself. He complains. He's always late. He's quick to criticize and judge. An awful listener. I went on and on." Coach turned to me and said, "Ok, Bob. That's all about you." What! I'd just given him ten things that got under my skin. And he says, It's all about Me?

Here's what followed.

"Bob, you can't change one molecule in your friend's body. He might change. But you cannot change him. You can only change you." Okay, I was done with this guy. Chris made no sense. If I was going to continue with him, we had to resolve this. We spent a month. Four one-hour sessions finding what it was about me, my behaviors, and my reactions that contributed to the conflict. Why wouldn't I discuss with my friend how I felt? Rather than allow things to fester. I had to make myself vulnerable. Put the relationship at risk to make things better. What was I afraid of? What was it about me I had to change?

I faced the risk I was avoiding. Instead of swallowing hard every time I was with him, I had to change myself. My reaction to his behaviors. Hard for me to put words to all this, but I *did* change. I stopped being a martyr. Stopped being a victim of his issues. And I watched him change in response to my changes. I relaxed more when being with him... the conflict subsided. The best way to improve my relationship with this guy was to change me. Not try to change him. I changed and realized what Chis had told me from the beginning....

"Bob, it's always about you."

Grasping the fact that you only control you. Your behavior. Your responses. Your decisions. You only change others, any situation by taking action or not. By deciding when to engage and when not to. It's never about what the other guy or gal needs to do. That's up to them. Not you. It's always about you.

The early lesson here. Connecting is first accepting everything begins with you and then taking responsibility. It's All About "You." Have I said this enough times for you?

# The Thread

*The following piece reinforces my previous message. Taking personal responsibility is key to personal growth. God meant for us to be faithful, confident, and loving. Here's the common "thread" woven through my entire career as a coach. That which "connects" us all is connected by what follows.*

A month before my 75th birthday, a good friend of mine asked me if he could help me celebrate! At lunch one day, he asked me this, "You've coached hundreds of people over decades. Is there a common 'thread' you can identify in each of them? A key to all your interactions with them over so many years?" Wow! What a profound question to ponder. I'd have to search my mind, my remembrances, and see. Get back to him.

So, as is my custom. Early morning "quiet time." Music in the background. Today, Andrea Bocelli. People ask... "Why do you get up so early?" As I said, there are "fireflies" that flicker early for attention. A gesture I need to extend to another. The daily text I send to my grandchildren. Ideas about a few things I might do today to have a positive impact on others.

What was the common "thread?" I started going through the rolls. Those I'd managed, led, or coached. The occasions I'd helped someone with a challenge or confusion... all of their issues were so varied. John, Susan, Steve? Successes, failures. Accomplishments. Personal goals and objectives? Changes in behavior. None of these were common to all. Nope. Couldn't come up with a common "thread." Then one morning while making coffee, it came to me. Startled. Taken aback. Where did this "message" come from? A "firefly" right before my eyes. That was it! This was the "thread."

The Bible says, "Love thy neighbor as thyself." How many Sundays have I said these words? Practicing what's offered here needs to be restated. "Love thyself as you love your neighbor." Love thy neighbor? Sure. But if we are to do so, "as thy self" must come first. I was onto something. A couple of sips of coffee. My favorite every morning chair. *Was this really it? The "thread?"* I went back to the rolls... one by one. Yes. This was it. Let me offer you an illustration.

Take Joe. Not his real name. A successful guy. On paper... he leads an enchanted life. When I began coaching Joe, we had trouble connecting. He told me everything in his life was good. So well in place. Then why was he with me? If everything was going so well? Why me? Why now? He hemmed and hawed when I questioned him. *Surely a guy this accomplished couldn't be this indecisive*, I thought.

24

Then I asked him the question that revealed all. This was the common "thread." *Joe, do you love yourself?"* He looked at me with a searing eye contact I'd not seen before. Without hesitation, he emphatically replied, *"No."*

This was the "thread." Joe needed to love himself. "As thyself" He did not. I repeated this to myself as I worked with him. If Love is the key to all, the freedom to choose love above all else is crucial. Love within us. You must embrace it. Love you first.

*Self-love. The "Thread." The one thing commonly crucial for us all to realize. Why? Because your capacity to love yourself determines the degree to which you are then able to love others.*

So, at last... the "Thread"... *Self-love.* Love of self. Ask yourself this question. "Do I love myself? Before loving my neighbor. Some feel a little selfish when this question comes up. Is this self-serving? Even a little arrogant to think about. No. Love is the greatest gift of all. God lives within us all. You are a "thumbprint." There is only one of you. God created you in his image. You must love you – yourself, first.

An important discovery. *Self-love.* This was the common "thread" woven through all those relationships. Until you love yourself... loving your neighbor will fall short.

The first section of this book focuses on taking personal responsibility for your life. Living as an adult. We are born into childhood. We migrate to adolescence. Some of us can get "stuck" in either of these. (I've coached 45-year-old children) Perspective, self-awareness, and wisdom all fuel your journey. Your decisions are the guideposts that lead you on your way.

As James Allen wrote in his book in 1902, _As a Man Thinketh_, "As you see your life, so shall it be. Grow weeds or flowers... the choice is yours." Once again. Accepting that life is always about "You" is a good start. "Connects" you with you more. But don't expect this to be an instant transformation. *Self-love,* while it's the "thread," takes patience, time.

# WHO ARE YOU...
# REALLY?

*Let's take a magnifying glass and look
more closely at the question... "Who Are You... Really?"*

Connecting YOU with YOU begs the question: "Who Are You?"

You think you know you. I think I know *me*. But this may be only partially true. Let me share a few thoughts.

I wrote a piece in this book called *"The Deep Pool Within."* Picture an immense dome... the size of the earth. All of us are living on top of it. We scurry. We hurry. We do a lot of stuff. The more we do, the better we feel. Right? Being busy is one way we validate ourselves. The top of the dome is a blur... a pure rush of activity. Beneath the dome is a deep, fathomless pool. It houses who we are... really. Our spirits. Our subconscious minds. Our souls. Where God is silently calling us to be. A belief that inspired me to ask, *"Who Are You? Really."*

One of the key concepts throughout this book is FOCUS. Much of what I share here is aspirational. Values, desires, purpose. Behaviors. Things unseen that are critical for personal growth to occur. In order benefit from what I've written, you must focus. Select key parts of that strike you most. Takeaways. Write 'em down! Always remember. *"The weakest pencil stroke is better than the strongest memory."* Focusing... keeping a record of your takeaways will make a vast difference.

Every coaching process I conduct involves first learning about the person sitting in front of me. I make my observations. They make their own. But to get a true picture of who they are... really? We have to reach out to people who know my coachie well. Those who have seen him/her in a clear light. In most cases, for years.

Here's an exercise I conduct to learn more about who is in front of me.

Pick six people in your life you trust implicitly. Who you know will be brutally honest with you. Ask them to do this...

*"Send me an email and tell me the things you see about me that work... and those you see that don't."*

This takes courage... vulnerability on your part. But it's always revealing. A great way to "see" who you are from the perspectives of those close to you, who know you well.

They will tell you how great you are. The things that work well. How much they love you. Then they'll startle you with the things they see about you that don't work well. Usually "blind spots." Things they see about you that you don't see about yourself. All this feedback lands close to home. Can even be a bit depressing. *"I didn't know you felt that way."* Most times, this provides us with potential changes, opportunities for growth, and for the coaching ahead. Areas where the coachie chooses and needs to improve.

This process is effective when beginning a coaching process.

Stop for a moment and consider how important the decisions we make in life are. The friends you make, the spouse you choose, the career you pursue. What is it that determines your path? Reveals to you the core of who you really are. Think about this. What we project to others daily is masked most of the time. Not who we really are. More who we think we should be. How we would like others to see us. We adapt to the circumstance and relationships around us. It's just human. But when you allow others to see who you really are, you project a clear image, an authentic picture of yourself for others to see.

Probing more deeply to know yourself is never easy. But, opening yourself to new possibilities connects you to new sources of energy to drive you forward. Magical... thus the value of engaging in the exercise above.

I always remember my father-in-law. He was a superb judge of character. When he got to know someone who was comfortable with who they were, he'd always comment, *"She's real. She's for real."* He could always see through someone's "mask." Get to who they really were... quickly.

*"How are you?"* The always well-intentioned greeting when we first meet someone? The usual response. *"I'm great."* Now, I'm not saying there is anything wrong with this. But we all have "stuff." *"I'm great"* is usually short of the truth. I'm just saying most of us rarely reveal our true selves when opening a conversation. Makes sense. But revealing what's beneath the surface? What's in our "deep pool?" Well, most rarely go there. Not saying one should dump their bucket at the outset of a conversation. It's just refreshing when someone trusts me enough to talk about their real "stuff."... Even when first meeting them.

My reflections yield these thoughts.

Consider three questions...

Our behaviors and motives intertwine, but rarely are they totally aligned. Motives are our true drivers. Those parts of us beneath the surface in that "deep pool" that hold our true feelings... desires. Behaviors are reflections.

The way we choose to filter our true motives. Go out into the world allowing others to see us... but not as who we really are. Rather, who we would like to be.

True or not?

So, we behave. Are our behaviors misaligned with our motives? Wanting to be liked leads us to act more amiably around others. To please. Give others what we think they want? We want others to see us as smart, together, navigating life successfully. While normal, this may prevent us from revealing our true selves - from being fully authentic. We want others to see us as who we want to them see. Not as we really are.

True or not?

Acknowledging the concepts above allows you to uncover more of the real you. How you can best manage yourself. Am I being true to who I want to become? Or am I limited unnecessarily by other influences? Along the way. To be someone else.

True or not?

Do you know? "Who You Are... Really?"

# The Movie

*So far, I've suggested taking responsibility in life is crucial for healthy living. You are responsible. Everything is about you. Knowing yourself better, more authentically, is what needs to follow. By answering the question... Who Am I Really? Clarifying who you are can take months... even years. Through working with a coach, therapist, mentor, or confidant? There's no "do-it-yourself" option available here. As you realize that taking responsibility for You is foundational to living a productive life. Strive to know more about who you are. You can begin your journey. This is an excellent way to realize that you have the power to direct the energy that drives your life. Find the frequency that best fits you.*
*Just one more way to harmonize the way you travel your life path.*
*Imagine your life is like a movie...*

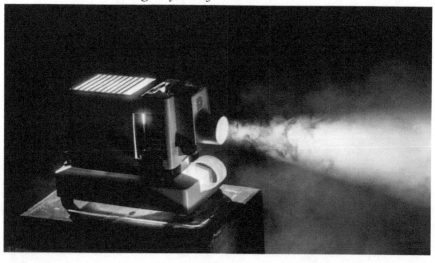

*Life is like a movie playing before your eyes. And you get to write the script.* That's right. You write the script.

The network of energy... the focus of this book. Operates every second. Can you impact what happens each day? Can you "write" the script of what's playing before your eyes? Direct the flow of energy surrounding you?

A couple of examples to make my point here...

My first...

A friend of mine spent some time playing pro golf. His stroke average was only a shot and a half less than the top twenty-five players on the PGA tour. Yet he was an "also ran." Didn't last a year.

When I asked him the difference between his game and tour leaders, he replied... "Putting. I can get the ball tee to green with the best. It's the putting that separates us." He continued, "Take Tiger. Most of the players on tour? When they putt? They 'hope' the ball into the hole. Tiger 'wills' the ball into the hole."

Part of Tiger's magical lure. The world's fascination with how he plays the game of golf. Tiger "wills" the ball into the hole. Tiger Woods writes his own "script." An aura of energy surrounds him. Muhammad Ali... Michael Jordan. Larger-than-life figures who, through their sheer force of will, focus, and determination, wrote their own "script." And yes, to a great extent, they "controlled" the network of energy around them.

**My second example...**

Maybe less grand than the first, but no less illustrative of my point. My granddaughter is a very determined young lady. At age ten, she was playing bingo at the club our family belongs to. There were twenty-five or so players in the room. She was the youngest by far. I watched her as each number was called. Struck by the intensity of her gaze, I asked her, "Are you okay, honey?" She looked up and replied, "PopPop, I'm going to win."

She returned to her gaze. As the numbers were called, I noticed she didn't blink. Her stare was stunning.

She won three of four games. At ten years of age, her "script" was clear to her.

And you say?

"Oh my God, Bob. Are you kidding me? That was nothing more than a coincidence. You've lost it."

Ok, but my experience has proven to me the presence of my own "script"... written for good or bad. I used to do a lot of public speaking. Energy was so defining of how my talks went. It was the barometer of how I did.

In the public speaking world, there is a term called "pin drop."

If you want to take the temperature on how a talk is going? Pause in the middle for a couple of seconds... and listen. Are feet shuffling? Can you see some in your audience on their phones? Maybe even a few walking out? Or can you feel a stillness? A total lack of movement in the crowd. All eyes on you. If it's the latter... you've achieved "pin drop." If a pin dropped in row fifteen, you would hear it.

My "pin drop" speeches would end with applause... many times standing ovations. Those absent the "pin drop"? Usually polite applause.

I wrote the script. Controlled the energy in the room.

Stick with me. The "movie" I attempt to create here has just started. So much more to follow. The network of energy that connects us all is at work at this moment.

### So far, I've offered:

• "It's All About You" taking responsibility. Know that regardless of circumstance, determining your role in what life sends your way is crucial. You're never a victim.

• "Who You Are" stresses the need for authenticity. Being bold. Seeing who you really are. There's the public persona. Then there's the real you. A process. Not a snap of the fingers.

• "The Movie" playing before your eyes. Its script is far more within your control than you may realize. Energy at your fingertips you can direct... even control.

# The Lens

*Now let's consider the "Lens" through which the previous concepts may be channeled. How you choose to see the events in life. Your focus. The lens you peer through. How you choose to see them? Can be an important determinant of how your life unfolds.*

Is your life like a movie playing before your eyes?

Is the "movie" simply what we see? Just what it is? Or is this something over which we have some control? Does energy play a part here too?

When I moved from Connecticut to Atlanta in 1990, I was anxious about the move. I wondered why. I'd had great success in Connecticut. Nancy couldn't wait to throw all her winter clothes away. Move to the South. But I was edgy. I usually was. Just now more than usual. Then one day it came to me. Moving from the North to the South would be a real cultural change. The North and South were so different, I thought. This concerned me. Could I relate, adjust to the people there? Fit into my new home?

So, I had lunch with a mentor. An old friend of mine who I met for advice or a mental boost from time to time. I often felt lonely while leading my business in CT. He'd been a great sounding board. Helped me restore my confidence. Always had great perspectives. A true wisdom guy.

*"I need your help with something, Karl. I'm moving to Atlanta to build another business. I'm concerned. People in the South are much slower. And I don't think they're as smart as we are up here in the North. I'm not sure I'm going to relate well to them. My business life down South may be so different and difficult."*

Now Karl is one of the best listeners on earth. He never provides an instant response to any question. Lifting his eyes over his reading glasses, he stared at me, paused for five seconds, and said, *"Bricks? If that's how you see them? That's how they'll be."*

The Lens. My lens would determine how I saw my new home. How I chose to view the people there. The movie would play out. It was up to me to write the script. What I saw through my lens was my choice. My perception would be my reality.

What a comfort Karl's wisdom proved to be.

Such an important life lesson. Our attitude, our perception of life experiences are all choices we make. We choose the lens through which we see things. I remembered another thing Karl reminded me of once. *"You see things are bad? Or you see things are good. Either way, you're right,"*

We moved to Atlanta shortly after my lunch with Karl. Man, were my new clients and friends great! They may live life a little "slower" in the South... but I found they live life a bit "softer" than my friends up North.

And no... I was not smarter than my Southern friends.

This was a great way to open a new chapter

Helping people grow is my life's mission. I currently have eight people I coach. One of the most effective coaching tools I employ goes like this: My coachie faces a challenge. Many times a very daunting one. His first reaction? "I can't possibly do this. I just can't."

My response is always, *"You need to refocus your lens. Think about this. You're viewing a challenge as a climb up an impossibly steep hill. The reality? Refocus your lens, and it will be like piercing a veil and walking through it.*

How many times have you faced something... saying to yourself, "Oh, I could never do that!" But somehow you decide to take the risk. You venture out and try. Not knowing what the outcome will be. Amazing. You find you were wrong. This was doable. The challenge wasn't as difficult as you thought it would be. Your illusion of something impossible had been a perception that wasn't the reality.

You refocused your lens... and grew the strength to prevail. What a wonderful life lesson.

The message here?

I'm not suggesting you take on challenges recklessly. Calculated risk is always preferable. But "either you think you can, or you think you can't, either way, you're right." Change things by changing your attitude. Refocus the lens through which you view challenges. You will write the script that will play before your eyes based on the focus of your lens.

By now, a picture should be emerging. Connecting with yourself is the greatest of all connections. Taking full responsibility for all that happens in your life. Accepting that you are in charge of how you view things... everything around you? This is the foundation for understanding the incredible network of energy that fuels and directs life. You build confidence as you realize this is true. Are all things within our control? Of course not. But how we perceive them... how we choose to respond to them? Yes. This is in our control. Now... how can you prepare yourself for this reality? Mentally, spiritually... even physically. Amidst the myriad of connections that guide us through life's experiences, knowing how to discipline yourself and accept the invisible? Is an absolute.

# Discipline

*So, check this out.*

*"Self-control: Orderly or prescribed conduct;
an organized pattern of behavior."*

There are a lot of things that we propose and we execute far less. We
visualize those "home runs" in life that will magically change everything.
But progress in almost every endeavor is driven by smaller commitments.
Incremental steps. "Singles" and "Doubles." Try hitting these first. Wow!

*The "homers" follow. This piece stresses the need to apply yourself to the work ahead. Stick with me. This is like a fine orchestra. I may be the conductor... but you make all the music. Discipline you? You'll do just fine.*

An important characteristic of successful people I've worked with... Discipline. The determination to do what one commits to doing. Simply doing what you say you're going to do. We all know what we need to do, even in most cases, how to do it. But it takes discipline to actually get things done.

Decades ago, Albert E. N. Gray, a professor at Temple University, conducted a multiyear study on what made the most successful people in life... successful.

Here's what he found:

*"Successful people form the habit of doing things that failures don't like to do. Don't do."*

Guilt, excuses, apologies, all the "I'm sorrys"... "The dog ate my homework." I've heard 'em all. People pay me a lot of money to guide them. I'm always amazed at how some piss away thousands of dollars with little to show for it. There just are those who are accountable... and those who are not. Separates the "men from the boys."

I make a "contract" with each person I coach that goes something like this. *"You can stop our work together at any time. In the middle of a sentence if you choose to. But know this, so can I. If you don't execute. Don't do what you say you will do, I can stop, too."* It's about a disciplined path to move forward. A decision to grow. Or not.

Another key to disciplined behavior is note-taking. Writing things down. When I coach, it's usually an early indicator of disciplined behavior or not. A coachie takes notes during our sessions or not? Revealing. Few of us have a photographic memory. Most of what we hear will drift into the ether if not grasped. Like "fireflies," thoughts will disappear if not captured in the moment.

I consider myself to be a disciplined person. I may write too much down. But what I've found? When I record a thought or an idea, it clears "thought space" in my mind for the next one. Makes me set deadlines, priorities... calendar things to get done. Discipline. I have folders on my computer for each person I coach... save folders for those who've moved on. Years later, a coachie may return to work with me. I never want to begin again from scratch. An integral part of my value is knowing, remembering the details of our earlier work... professionally, and personally.

This allows me to build a constructive, cumulative process with a coachie. Learn to review the past and plan forward. What's next after two weeks have passed? Names, commitments, accountabilities. When someone knows you won't forget, it's interesting how much more disciplined they become.

Discipline comes in many forms. It's not always a mechanical process. Some are successful in working this way. Others are more erratic. They move quickly, more randomly, through their thoughts. Take a more indirect path that works for them. But my measure is always the result. It's always the final measure. It's not about the means... It's about the end.

We are creatures of free will. Change is a choice, not a matter of capacity. So discipline. But as I began this piece, discipline in whatever form it shows up will always be essential for any process to succeed... coaching or otherwise.

# TRY NOW AND NEXT

*The process of personal growth is incremental. This next post may say it best. Hit the singles and the doubles first. The home runs will follow. Growth is a process... not an event. A marathon... not a sprint. Read this next one. You'll get the message.*

Norman Lear is the genius creator of several fabulous television series. "All in the Family"; "Maude"; "The Jeffersons" are among his best. In an interview a few years ago, at age 96, he was asked, "Mr. Lear, you've been immensely successful. Has there been one key as to why?" Lear replied,

*"Oh, yes. I've lived my life focused on one simple adage. All I have today are two things... "now and next."*

Makes me think of where we are now on January 1, 2021. We are in the "Now" and we are looking for what's "Next." Struggling. Our "Now" carries a lot of weight as we enter each new year. We're burdened, heavy with the dramatic twists and turns... wrenchings really from the year past. But the human spirit may best be described in a poem by the great Carl Sandberg. I paraphrase with license here.

*"The human spirit is like an old anvil... grinning at all the broken hammers."*

We always seem to find the resolve to reach out for our "Next."

I've found the best sign of future performance is past performance. The "anvil" in us has always stared down those "broken hammers." Depression; war; economic collapse. We've always responded... resiliently! Picked up that next hammer.

It's our human nature to fear the unknown... we are naturally anxious about what the future holds. Of course, if there's no anxiety in not knowing what's next, there can be no such thing as a resilient response. Right? How do I see this time, this juncture in our lives? Jan 1, 2021? An opportunity to reset... summon the God-given deep well of strength in us all... shine up that old "anvil" and go forth. Maybe like never before. Toward what's "Next."

Let me continue... although I diverge somewhat.

It's customary with each new year to make resolutions. Aspirations regarding weight, reading, career... changes in behavior. Most of these efforts fade soon after we make them. We usually are good at describing "what and how." Rarely do we spend enough on the real motivator of change. The "Why" of what we want to, what we intend to do.

I've worked with many well-meaning people who commit to change. "Who am I? Who do I want to become?" But human nature is like Nike, they want to "Just do it!" Fast. Want it all... Now. Usually bound to fail. Why?

M. Scott Peck wrote one of the famous books of our time, The Road Less Traveled. Among the many incredible lessons Peck offers is the concept of "delaying gratification." Scott's suggestion? Life is like eating cake. Do you eat the cake first? Or the icing first? Most of us are "icing" people. We probably know we should eat the cake first. But... mmm... that icing just looks too good.

He further offers that eating the cake first makes that icing so much sweeter. "Just do it!" Go for the icing? Pass on the cake? You may invite failure.

Perhaps the pandemic gifted us in a slightly bizarre way. All those things that gave us such great satisfaction were on hold. "Delayed" beyond our control. Hey, we didn't even get to eat the cake! Much less the icing!

Now, when we see some of the old "normal" return, the cake and the icing seem to be so, so, so much sweeter!! Because we went so long without either? Delayed gratification has its unexpected rewards. How 'bout that!

One thing Norman Lear didn't say. Between his "Nows" and his "Nexts" was... time. "Space" when he assessed Why... he would move to his next "Next." At first, Lear appears to be an "icing" guy. No. Lots of "cake" before the "icing" in his "Nows" and "Nexts."

Opening every new year is a gift. As an old friend of mine used to say, "Hats off to the past! Coats off to the future!" There are only two types of people who address the issues posed here... Those who do something about it, and those who don't.

So, how will you be different looking ahead? The pandemic years were unique in that there was so much we lost, moved away from. But your "Nows" and "Nexts" will require lots of cake before getting to the icing. Moving too quickly to restore what we lost during COVID might create new problems for us.

# CHAPTER 2
# SPIRITUALITY

# SPIRITUALITY

There may be no stronger connection between us than that created through our shared spirituality. Across the planet... whether through formalized religion. Or belief there is a higher power in charge. The Spirit, however, interpreted, underpins our existence.

I remember the story of an executive of a large company in DC. He had studied all the phases of life. He wanted to validate the role spirituality played while moving through each phase.

He traveled to South Asia to learn more about spirituality. What was it like across our world? He met with a spiritual guru in India for three full days. He was mesmerized by what he learned. The guru described life's phases in exactly the same way he had envisioned them back home. Thousands of miles away, each phase was magically similar.

I like to think of our spiritual journey in life as a cycle. We travel on an undefinable path that we know is real but hard to grasp. As I open this chapter on spirituality, I want to paint a picture of things that inspire our spirituality.

# The Deep Pool Within...

*I referred earlier to your "deep pool." I begin this section by asking you to think deeply. Feel that part of yourself that lies beneath the surface. Your true loves, your passions. Your wants, your dreams. Try to view this part of you as fuel for living. The essence of who you are.*
*There is indeed a deep pool within you to "drink" from.*

Sight... sound... smell... taste... touch. Our five senses. Today is fast. A blur, at times. When do we pause? Stop to savor these five senses? The spaces between all those notes? Not often. The events, the pressures, the demands of life consume us. Is this our future, too?

But imagine your senses. Linked with what we hear and say, every day amidst all the "noise" out there. Try to view all this activity sitting on the surface of a very large dome. You know... like the dome atop an Italian cathedral. Just huge. Earth-size. All that activity, The blur life offers each day. All of us... scurrying on top of the dome. Chaotic, at times. This is our everyday existence.

Now picture a vast space... a reservoir-like pool under the dome. The senses, alive, vibrant... even more so. Instinct, caring, love of others, love of life. Residing there... ever so quietly. But ever so ever-present.

Here lies a silent, almost dormant part of us residing in this deep pool beneath. A vast reservoir under the dome. The subconscious? That's part of it. But something we rarely touch, rarely dip into. You might refer to this as your true inner thoughts. Your true desires. Feelings. All the love to be tapped into or not. The part of you that you access when slowing down. Ask yourself, "Why am I here?' You're settled. Affirming your values, aspirations, love for self, and others. Again, when you're quiet, alone. *Wh this really about? Who am I? What is God calling me to be?* The deep pool within. That's where this is. Only here do you actually find truth... fuel for growth.

Your pool can be cloudy... even dark. Filled with bad stuff... thoughts and feelings that never serve you well. Envy, hatred, anger, deceit, regret, sorrow, evil, at times. Not a healthy pool to draw from. Or it can be clear and bright. Filled with cleansing thoughts and feelings like love, empathy, charity, humility, integrity, strength of character. Although silent... under the surface, this fathomless deep pool lies well beneath the dome. Well... it actually has a lot to do with your destiny. Who you become. To illustrate... consider two people with diametrically opposing "pools." I feel I should apologize for comparing these two. But each lived extremely different lives.

Charles Manson... dark pool. Mother Teresa... bright pool. Destinies they created. Forever etched in our memories. One, the essence of evil, hatred. The other? Nothing but loving grace. Goodness. Some access their pool through prayer. Others meditate. Some will just spend quiet time with themselves. Still, others will do none of these.

At the core of all of this? Something God-given. The power of choice. Your choice. What will your deep pool look like? You are the creator. How you live life is... always your choice. It's all about you.

You enjoy life for sure. But you also need be conscious of where you're going, where you're headed. The quality of your pool beneath? There's a balance here. Attend to the "now" things in life for sure. All those things atop the dome. But also set aside time to ponder *What's next? Who am I? What am I being called to do?* Slowly dip into your pool. Draw from it the things that work for you. Clarify your values. Live them.

Whatever messages come to you... repeat them to yourself. Over and over. Blend your day-to-day activity with a little self-examination. Find a few "spaces between the notes." Quiet yourself. Allow the deep pool within you to guide you... direct you on the best path forward.

# The Deeper
# You've Been

*Reaching... calling on the spirit from a deep pool brings to mind:*
*How do you put it all to work. Build strength from it.*
*In fact... the deeper you dive into the "pool"*
*the more you drink from its magical source of spiritual strength.*

*The Deeper You've Been... the higher you go.* What do I mean by "Deeper?" Take Abraham Lincoln and Oprah Winfrey. Both came from lowly backgrounds... In Oprah's case? Poverty-stricken. You've heard the stories. A one-room home for six. Abuse. Misfortune. Sexual dysfunction. Lincoln suffered from acute episodes of depression while in office as President.

Whatever their circumstance, so many of the greatest among us, have gone "deep." Met the most challenging of life experiences. Only to emerge and rise "high." Above it all. Higher because they started in life... deep. But then chose to grow and rise higher. Move from the deep... to the higher in response to their challenges.

Physical exercise is good for you. Makes you feel better. About yourself. About your health. Got it? What we can't miss, however, is how mental and spiritual exercise does the same for us... but in more subtle ways. Our psyche, our attitude... our countenance all change when we exercise our mind and spirit to work our way through life's challenges.

I went to a parent-teacher conference years ago at the school in Connecticut my two daughters attended. A question raised by a concerned parent? "Why does my child have to study algebra? It will have no practical use in the real world." Our impeccable headmaster at the time replied, "Respectfully, if your child disciplines himself to work through the challenge of algebra, there's a benefit. When he arrives at those courses of more interest to him... his learning and enjoyment will accelerate. Be more meaningful because he worked hard... gutted his way through algebra." Go deep? Go higher.

All the challenges in life are at their core exercises of the mind and spirit. So, just like our bodies... we need to embrace, appreciate... be grateful even when our butts are getting kicked. Good! Challenges abound! They exist to strengthen you... Be thankful for them! You are far more resilient than you know.

The Lincolns, the Winfreys of today have gone "Deep"... into their prior life experiences and have chosen to go "High." Higher because they never martyred, never saw themselves as victims. Just because the first hand dealt them was empty, they still moved forward with passion, confidence, and determination, becoming role models. So, the next time you feel you're in a tough spot... stop and think. Hmmm... is this meant to strengthen me? Yes. It's the mental, spiritual "muscle building" you need to get into shape for all that better stuff ahead. Algebra is good! Go "Deep?" Go "Higher." We need to see life as having no struggles... only challenges.

Welcome them. Embrace them. They're a gift. Be sure you go deep. Ever deeper. Because the deeper you've been, the higher you'll go.

# "Centering Down"...
# Your Safe Place

*I've found an exercise described below that takes me to a "safe place" where just "being" can fuel the spirit. By "centering down", I allow my spirit to flow more easily. Remove the barbs and difficulties of daily life for a brief time. And yes... give me rest.*

I listened to a wonderful interview this morning with Robert Franklin, former president of Morehouse College and Visiting Professor at Stanford University's Martin Luther King, Jr. Research and Education Institute.

Dr. Franklin opened with this:

"We're facing a moral crisis in America today. Driven by the loss of our sense of humanity, consumed in the belief that our own self-interest, our own needs always prevail over the needs of others. We all seem to have our own "micro" value system. Always living in righteousness. "I'm right. You're wrong." Consumed by our own sense of self-importance, intoxicated by the feeling that we sit in the center of the universe. Taking ourselves too seriously." I agreed.

But then Dr. Franklin's message drew me to this:

This excess of self-absorption leads to a disconnection between us.

Amidst the chaos is an epidemic of stress. Some I coach have shared how much going to sleep serves as an escape, relief from the pressures that plague them. Some have taken their need for relief further... even faint thoughts of suicide. Shocks me.

Take Jane (pseudonym). She'd had a horrific childhood. Abuse. Emotionally abandoned by her parents. Now in her mid-thirties, she was married to a great guy. One beautiful child. But Jane couldn't slow down. Despite my pleas. The concept of "slowing down to speed up" evaded her. Anxiety, illusions of despair gripped her daily. She simply could not rest... slow herself mentally.

It was during the interview that Dr. Franklin offered two words that truly lit my fire. Gave me a path Jane might pursue to find some relief. Soften some of the intensity that consumed her.

The concept of "centering down."

"Traveling" mentally, spiritually to our God-given selves. A method of self-control that has been a wonderful "escape" for me personally. Might be for Jane, too.

Let me explain.

I see my own experience of "centering down" as a reaching inward to soothe my soul... vibrate my self-consciousness. Providing me an opportunity to retune, realign my actions with my values. A "centering down" exercise. It always seems to recenter me.

A simple process of meditation, prayer, quiet time with oneself. An opportunity to travel to other parts, levels of me not present in the day-to-day.

It usually goes like this...

Eyes closed. Shoulders relaxed. Thoughts as empty as possible. Absent the usual "noise." Breathing deeply, slowly. Rhythmically. A feeling of moving into a slight hypnotic state.

The feeling for me? Like I'm slowly descending in a small elevator. 3-2-1... counting myself down. Moving to the next level of my consciousness. Opening my senses. Feeling a connection within me beneath the everyday flurry of life.

When "centered", I visualize what I call my "safe place." A mental... spiritual process creating a picture of my favorite place on earth. A spiritual landing of sorts.

This can be a place you visited... a place you've vacationed to... even something as simple as your backyard. Just a place you can retreat and... rest. Be only with you. Be alone.

My "safe place?"

Always on the ocean. Sound of wind and soft chirps of gulls. A huge, sun-drenched cliff to my right. Spots of foliage scattered over its massive wall. A beach of the finest sand I've ever been on. White as snow. No footprints.

The ocean is always magical. Seemingly endless. The wind lifts small waves glistening with spray as the sun reflects on them. Rows and rows of waves. Moving toward shore. Each patiently waits its turn to roll onto the beach. Over and over. The soft rolling sound of waves coming into shore. So quieting, so restful.

This is my "safe place." My refuge... my place to hide. Just to be with myself. A vivid description... right? I've traveled to my "safe place" many, many times.

Jane has adopted this exercise. Still challenged. But diligently, she repeatedly visits her "safe place." Sitting on a dock at her home on a beautiful lake. As we conduct our sessions over the phone, I feel her voice soften. Her speech slows some. Gives me confidence she is making progress.

"Centering down." Slowly visualizing. Moving to a "safe place." A refuge. Dispelling illusions (perceptions that aren't reality) that may stress you in the flurry of everyday life. Just a little comfort... a soothing pause. Takes maybe five to ten minutes. That's all.

You may have no urgent crisis needing relief like Jane. But this is a beautiful way to clear the air. Rest. Simply be. Where is your "safe place"? Try to go there. First time may feel a bit awkward. Hard to "see." But as you repeat the process, watch. The picture will brighten.

"Centering Down" has become a good friend to me.

# It's No Secret

*What's the one thing that most makes life wonderful?*

I reconnected with my coach yesterday. He's always got something new or something we return to that has added impact to my personal growth. He asked me this question. *"Bob, what is the one thing we most crave in life?"* I fumbled through. Success? Joy? Appreciation from others... respect?"

He replied, *"Well, those things may bring it to you. But they are not the one thing we crave above all else. It's no secret... that one thing is... Intimacy."*

Typical guy thing. I immediately went to images of sex. *"Yes, sex can be intimate,"* he said. *"It is one of God's greatest gifts. But this is not my message here."* Coach continued. *"Intimacy can be found and experienced in so many unexpected, less obvious places. God intended this to be so."*

Think of a time a loved one has looked into your eyes and spontaneously told you, "I love you." Or when a dear friend reaches out to you for help. And your interaction closes with a deep and lasting hug. Or when you awaken in the morning in a favorite place. An ocean view. Overlooking a mountain range. Or simply walking through a forest. These, too, are/can be *intimate* experiences. If you choose to accept them, see them as so. As I've said before, I refer to these subtle flashes of awareness as "fireflies." Here for a moment, but fleeting. Reach out. Capture them before they're gone. *Intimate* moments can be like "fireflies" too.

I attend a restaurant regularly. A favorite waiter of mine came to my table the other day. He's from Haiti. A magnificent young man. *"Bobby, your birthday is tomorrow, and I want you to have this."* He reached into a small bag and pulled out a small onyx pyramid with glittering gold shavings inside. *"Bobby, you have been so kind to me. I want to give you this symbol that, according to Voudon doctrine, is the source of eternal energy."* We both teared up as he left the table. This had been an *intimate* moment for me... and him, too. Not necessarily grand. But without question... *intimate.*

My mother died eight years ago. Sometimes, I'll sit quietly in the morning. Try to return to the deep, loving feelings I had for her. I'll peer out a window, and suddenly see a red cardinal perched on a small branch. We don't have many cardinals where I live. It seems to look at me. Even smiling a little? I warm. Could this be Mom's spirit somehow trying to reach out to me? *Intimacy* felt here, too, for sure. I'll bet you've had a similar experience.

What I've learned over the years of working with my coach is that *intimacy is the essence of the joyous experiences in our lives.* But it's the less grand, less noticeable moments that touch us that can get us through an exhausting day or a challenging time. They can be small refreshers, reminders that our plight isn't so consuming after all. The Lord gives us "breathers." Such a blessing.

A wildly busy friend of mine refers to them as "diamonds." Another calls them "Benedictine Moments." Brief flashes of *intimacy* that make an enormous difference. My friend told of watching his oldest son walk an old, disabled woman across a busy street one morning. He took just an instant to stop and rest amidst the chaos or confusion. See the goodness in his son. An *intimate* "diamond" for him during a stressful day. We only have to be aware. Have the confidence these are "sent" our way. If only quietly... and many times imperceptibly.

But this is contrary to much of life's reality as our humanness pulls us in so many directions. Go, go... go! Do this! Do that! Finding those special moments when we can touch *intimacy* calls for a response opposite to how you're feeling, what you might be dealing with. A "space between the notes" pause. Knowing this can make all the difference.

As my day unfolds, I am open to those moments when a few small "diamonds" might come my way. Like the day my dear friend gave me that beautiful, glittering pyramid. They can be a source of eternal energy, too.

# FeeLING

*Can there be a moment more special than watching my granddaughter
spontaneously show her "feelings"
while playing at the ocean... dancing on the beach?*

Many years ago my coach told me, "Bob, you don't really *feel*." Huh?
I can cry at a Ford commercial. "No," he said. "You, and most of us, get
emotional. We don't really, truly *feel*. Feelings and emotions are different."
I've since learned he was right... here's how. Emotions are primarily our
response to outside stimuli. Movies, Hillary Clinton speeches, reading a

good book. Feelings are more internal. More heartfelt... Death of a loved one. Loss of a romantic relationship. Things that rock our being. Less on the surface. More visceral.

I had a conversation with a friend recently. Actually... a coaching moment. He was having several personal issues that were really weighing heavily on him. The most pressing was the death of his mother-in-law. The impact this had had on his entire family.

"We've all gone numb. We can't seem to move on." I told him the best thing he could do, all his family should do, was simply feel. Feel their feelings. Draw deep within and feel. Don't just emote. This is not an easy process to describe, let alone actually pull off. But truly feeling your feelings is one of the most important aspects of personal growth one can experience. Feeling amplifies sensitivity and empathy and may even make you a better listener. Helps you connect with others more genuinely. Most importantly, reconnect through the pain that is haunting you. As was the case with my friend and his family.

When you feel, you reach into the deepest part of yourself. Others will feel your sincerity. Believe me, it can be infectious. As I've mentioned, I used to do a lot of public speaking. Sometimes my speeches went well. Sometimes not. What I discovered was the times they didn't work; I was mostly emotional. Excited, tense, energetic. But things were different when I concentrated on how I "felt" my message. Projected from my heart vs my head. It was as though each member of my audience was in front of me... one on one. My feelings (energy really) connected with each person in the room. Resulting in a successful event.

So, think about it the next time you experience a rush or occasion when your emotions flow. Like the gift I feel when I see my granddaughter dancing on the beach. Will you emote? Or will you truly try to embrace the moment... allow your emotions to translate to deeper feelings? Takes practice. But I think you will find this to be very revealing... fulfilling.

# THE GATHERING

*Here's my personal vision of my spiritual destination. "The Gathering"*
*depicts how I hope to look back someday, ask myself the question...*
*"What was it all about?"*
*Why it's good for most of us to think about where we are going.*
*What's your destination?*

How would you like to create more in your life that would allow you to love yourself more? Here's my personal experience. Coachies frequently ask, "Coach, what's your preferred future? How would you like to be remembered?? Over many years, I've moved ever so slowly to define this for myself. Today, my preferred future is pretty clear. It's known simply as "The Gathering" Here it is:

I'm standing before an assembled crowd of family and friends. They are all standing on a series of concentric circled, narrow platforms. My family stands closest to me on the first circle. Others stand on other circles as they extend outward. I know all those on the rims well. They know me well, too. Each reminding me of a specific, personal journey or experience we've shared. The joys, the losses, the stumbles... the successes, and the failures. I tear up as I make eye contact with each one of them. From one to the next. Moving outward, connecting with them all from circle to circle to circle.

The presence of each person warms me. Captures my spirit, my heart. This is a "virtual" gathering of all my relationships. Those who have invited me into their lives, and allowed me to love them, guide them. Impact their lives. Each is unique. The love I have for one just amplifies the love I feel for the next. On and on... this is "The Gathering."

On my 75th birthday, a friend of mine and I had dinner. I've referred to this dinner in previous writings. Some business stuff to cover. But little did I know what else would ensue. He offered this. "Seventy-five years! Quite a milestone. Why don't I reach out to the many you've impacted over your life?" On reflection, I think my friend was a messenger, a "vessel" brought to assemble the many friends who had blessed my life. Even though I felt this might be a little self-serving, I relented, "Gosh, that would be amazing." We finished our dinner, and we moved on. Fast forward.

A FedEx box arrived the day before my 75th. A bound document inside. Sixty pages of best wishes, reflections. Stories. Thank yous. From all those who had gathered over years in my mind... my spirit. Right there on paper! My vision of the "Gathering" ... zoomed into my mind. Overwhelming... In front of me was the crystallization of my "preferred future." Thoughts, intense emotions rushed in as I read each message. Like reuniting with each person... "Oh wow, how are you? And you. And you!" So vivid as I relived my time with each of them.

No time had passed. My 75th birthday? My best! Not even close! I can never repay my friend for his precious gift. As I shared with one friend, "This was like attending my own funeral." He replied, "Yes, Bricks. May be true. The difference is, you're here to see how much you are truly loved." I've never felt so much so. My heartfelt thanks to each of you who sent your best wishes on my birthday. Helped me so fully celebrate my 75th birthday.

"The Gathering"... my picture of my end game. Today, I continue to strive to add others to the circles. What fun! Such a joyous... how can I best describe it? Obsession? Yeah!... I'm obsessed with the idea of expanding the number of those who might join "The Gathering."

*What might a "preferred future"... your "Gathering" look like for you?*

# THE POWER OF BELIEF

*If we had no doubt that God or another higher power exists, there would be no need for faith. No need to believe. The following is a post I wrote on an Easter Sunday. Says a lot about the power of belief.*

Nancy and I watched a movie the other day. "I Still Believe" won't win Academy Awards. But that on that afternoon for us? It was surely worthy of one. We piled a box of used Kleenex between us while viewing. A true, inspiring, and yet very sad story about a rising nineteen-year-old country music star, his loving girlfriend, and their life journey. A beautiful story of faith, grit, and love for one another. Laced with tragedy. Go see it.

Let me describe one scene in the movie that continues to resonate within me. Jeremy and Melissa, who is riddled with cancer, are dating. They go to visit a nearby planetarium. Sitting in the middle of a large oval-shaped room, the lights gradually dim. The dome ceiling slowly opens above them and a startling, glorious galaxy of stars appears. Like bright grains of sand glittering in the night. Melissa raises her eyes to the ceiling, "Jeremy, isn't it amazing knowing there are trillions of stars in the heavens? But only one. Only one of them is Earth." Then she said this. "And do you see that swirling passage over there opening the way to more? An endless, darkened cave. Right in the middle of the constellation. Beyond the trillions of stars, we can see... are countless more. Each millions or billions of light years away."

"But Jeremy, if all this indeed is God's creation... the most miraculous part here? For me? Knowing for sure that HE knows my name. I'm very ill... but I know how much He loves me. God knows me by my name." The camera then focuses on the heavens above as Melissa and Jeremy tearfully gaze at the countenance. The wonder... the miracle of it all. Ultimately, Melissa passes away. Leaving Jeremy remembering her delight in knowing... HE loves her so. HE knows her by her name.

On Easter Sunday, Christians around the world celebrate the miracle of our Lord and Savior, Jesus Christ. The Jewish honor God with Passover. Hindus, Buddhists have their own form of celebration. These traditions... Easter, for sure, have lasted for thousands of years. Remembrances as brilliant today as they were then. So what did I say to myself as I watched this unforgettable scene in "I Still Believe?" Here we are. Fighting the critical challenges of a pandemic. Fear, uncertainty... in too many cases, the devastation of death. The standard closing of most conversations... articles in papers? "Be safe."

When I hear these words? My thoughts turn to the heavens. Look at all those stars. The infinite existence of power, vastness, and might... beyond comprehension. Unable to conceive what I'm seeing, experiencing... I say this. "We are safe." Whether it be God or some other higher power. We can be confident that we on Earth are but one tiny particle of ALL THAT

IS. We can have faith. Find the safety here we urgently want and need to embrace. Through Him. Just as Melissa did.

Whatever faith we choose. Who knows when we will leave this life? Where He will take us. Probably somewhere out there. In the galaxy among the stars. We need not fear anything, knowing there is something so much larger than us. He always... will always be in charge. And above all... HE WILL KNOW MY NAME... all our names. Your name too.

So on this Easter Sunday... The Lord be praised.

# Small Gestures

*CONNECTIONS abound. Here is yet another experience where the spirit of a moment dominates all.*

I came across a very interesting person recently. Can't remember his name... just his story. He was a writer. A talented writer. Ambitious. Wrote for years... (kinda like me). I related to him. Big ideas. "I'll change the world with my writings!" He had great responses to his writings. "But I can't break through. My audience is just too small. I'm falling short. Even failing." Then there was "the article." A brilliant piece about the current political scene, How God was watching. God was doing wondrous things. Amidst the chaos. It was published in a less well-known magazine.

He got a call one day. "Hi, I'm Oprah Winfrey." Surely an imposter. Turns out... NOT! It was Oprah! "I was fascinated by your recent article. Would you be willing to come to California to be my guest interviewee on a podcast of mine?" He was stunned! "Of course!" He did. The interview was at first intimidating. But Oprah had an incredible ability to reach out calmly, instilling confidence in him instantly. When it ended, he asked Oprah how she reached such a huge audience... changed so many lives. Did so many big things.

Here's what Oprah told him. "You know, I used to think a huge audience on TV, a speech in front of thousands was my calling. Certainly, my early days as a rather homely daughter of a sharecropper defined my life as very "small." Never foreshadowed what my life would become. That is to say, if I could get through high school, my life would be complete. But at my young age, it was a blessing to be the recipient of a blessed... *small gesture.*

One day, my 5th-grade school teacher had our class in assembly on stage. She asked "the beautiful gal in the front row" to step forward. Surely she wasn't referring to me. She was! Oh my god, *she* was "the beautiful gal in the front row." *Someone thinks I'm beautiful!... Homely no more,*" I thought. Something changed in me. In an instant. Such a *small gesture* that changed me... forever. Five seconds, three words changed my life." Struck by this... suddenly, our writer's perspective on all his grand dreams and desires came rushing to him, hearing what Oprah had told him. One *small gesture* had changed her life. That teacher in five seconds... not knowing the impact of what she had done. Changed a life.

All of his far-reaching visions. Reaching vast audiences. Feeding his ego? Suddenly, they deflated like a popped balloon. *Maybe the simple gesture of helping a lady across a street. Listening to a young twenty-year-old girl with a career question. Small gestures* have an enormous impact... in ways we will never know. Just like Oprah's teacher.

A totally new reality emerged for our aspiring writer.

I moved from Philadelphia to Connecticut in 1981. They sent there me to resurrect a failing business. Two guys I worked with in Philadelphia stopped by and gave me a small cellophane pouch. In it was one minute mustard seed. "We want you to think of your new venture as a series of many *small gestures*. Like this mustard seed. Step-by-step. One after another." I remembered the Lord citing that the mustard seed can be the spark that can ignite great things. My friends' *small gesture* changed me in ways they will never know. Connecticut was a success. I still have that pouch. Went on to Atlanta. Built another place. Mustard seed on board. The young writer and I had both learned a critical lesson. *Small gestures* can change lives. Oprah's teacher never knew the impact she had on that "beautiful" little girl that day. Oprah's message to her podcast guest had changed him in ways she may never know. Just as that mustard seed from my friends changed me.

My writer friend? He went on to win a Pulitzer Prize. Not by trying to write an epic. But simply writing what was on his heart *simply* each and every day. And again that mustard seed? Thank you, Harry and John. *Small gestures*... we really don't need to think grand. All life's opportunities, and all those *small gestures* make grand differences in ways you will never know.

# LIGHT

*One aspect of life that we take most for granted is the Lord's gift of light. Every morning... every day he fills with light. We fill our homes with light. A beautiful day helps one's mood. Light... so assumed. So automatic. Every day.*

The front page of the Wall St. Journal this morning featured a picture of the sun. Our source of daily light and warmth. The word "light" has come to me a lot lately. Feeling light. From the Bible, "Let your light so shine before men..." A guiding ray of light from a lighthouse comes to mind. Light vs. dark.

I heard recently that an "enlightening" power surfaces when we make ourselves vulnerable. What happens when you crack a smooth enamel veneer? Your light shines through.

Light in the early morning. The brightness of a clear day. Even the light as a computer screen opens. I never take light for granted. I always open my coaching sessions taking measure of the energy, the light coming from my coachie. One has what we call his "Gibometer"... another assesses his level of "buoyancy." On a scale of 1-10... what's the level of the light coming through? Lets me know the tone needed for our coaching session as it begins.

A friend recently sent me a sermon given by David Brooks, famed author, at the Washington Cathedral on July 5th. His message, "Beauty in a Storm" brought forth a "light at the end of the tunnel" image for me. There is, there would always be light, beauty amidst the storm. If only we are open to seeing it. Look for it.

My grandson sent me this memory on my birthday last week. "PopPop, I remember when we were at the Little League World Series last year, and I looked sadly at the weather report for the day – 0% chance of rain. You turned to me and said, 'Jack, that means there is a 30% chance of sunshine.' A bright, sunny day followed. Light, like water, is free, plentiful.

What if we had to live our lives in darkness.? And suddenly, light appears. This miracle of light would stun us all. You have a choice every day. Will you see the light? Or will you see the darkness? I hope you'll choose the "light" every time.

# Your "Higher Self"

*There are times when I have a conversation with myself. You know... while daydreaming. Or venting frustration. But when I shared this with my coach? "Bob, did you know you have a 'higher self?' A spirit who looks out for you every second of every day."*

There is a beautiful quote from Charlie Brown. As Charlie looks to the heavens...

*"Perhaps they are not stars in the sky, but rather openings where our loved ones shine down to let us know they are happy."*

Such a comforting word picture. Especially for those who have recently lost a loved one. It interests me that the stars and the universe are "up there" above us all. Looking down upon us.

I do believe we are "spoken to." Every day. Almost always when we're in silence. "Whispers"... fireflies are always available to us. More formally, I learned years ago from my coach. My "Higher Self" sends these to me. I named "him" (although there is no gender) Ernest. Imprinted, laser-like in my mind and spirit one evening by a full wall portrait of Ernest Hemingway in a restaurant we visit often. Weird? Maybe... but impactful. This picture resonates, "whispers" to me every time I see it. What I imagine... seems to emerge from a fog, slowly. I have to be quiet, patient, still, and wait to hear the "whispering." Real for me? Absolutely!

You've noticed by now, if you've read a number of the pieces in this book, I am a great proponent of "silence." Finding those moments, short periods of time when you are just with yourself. Yes, reaching out to your "Higher Self." I was skeptical at first. No more. Try it.

# THE PARABLE OF THE SPOONS

*I just love this one. Don't know where it came from. Just remember, I used to emphasize the importance of teamwork... thinking of the other guy when working together. A great lesson for our kids... the "kid" in each of us. Enjoy this instructional piece.*
*A great reminder... of that which ultimately connects us all.*

    In ancient times, there lived two groups of people who lived in villages next to one another. Times were trying. Survival... existence was what most of life here was about. Food and water were scarce. They all lived in tattered clothing. All was just very challenging. One day, a "spirit" summoned all the villagers to journey up onto a steep, forested hill nearby. Mysteriously, when they arrived in a clearing, they found two huge vats, and enormous tanks. Each filled with the most aromatic, wonderful food they had ever seen. A potential, rare feast for two groups of people who had lived in poverty for so long. Maybe their prayers had finally been answered. The vast amount of food here could feed their entire villages for months!

All the villagers hurried and circled around both tanks. There was great excitement on their faces as they peered at and took in the wonderful aroma of the beautiful food below.

The first group circled one vat. Each villager received a six-foot-long spoon to reach into the wonderful food. This first group anxiously extended their spoons deep into the tank. But the spoons were long and rigid. Because the villagers were so close together, each could only grasp their spoon by the handle. As a result, no one could bring the food to their mouths. They found the food was beyond their reach. No matter how they tried, each villager simply could not maneuver their spoon to their mouth. Their anguish, the hunger grew intense.

The second group circled the other vat and encountered the same dilemma. Spoons were too long, too rigid. Food was out of reach. They, too, screamed in frustration. Unable to feed themselves, they suddenly discovered something miraculous.

One in their group turned slowly to another villager and extended his rigid spoon across the tank... carefully lifting it to his friend's lips. Voraciously, his friend consumed all he could eat. The others were stunned. They extended their spoons, offering food to those across from them. Smiles of delight abounded. And you guessed it... all had more to eat than they ever could have prayed for. The simple gesture of offering what they had themselves to another had saved the day. All enjoyed the feast that the "spirit" God had gifted them. The first group, amazed... now looked at one another excitedly and did the same. They reached out, offering their food to the others across from them. And yes, both villages lived and thrived happily thereafter...

*As Jesus said, "... and the second commandment is like unto it. Love thy neighbor as thyself."* The Parable of the Spoons.

# THE POWER OF LOVE

*You'll note so many of my writings focus on the presence of love...
all around us. Here's another one.
Energized, sent to me by my great friend Jack Rogers.*

I'm an Episcopalian. Don't even know why I opened this piece with this sentence. It was top of mind, I guess. Maybe because I just finished reading the first thirty-six pages of a small book entitled, "The Power of Love." A great guy... dear friend, sent it to me yesterday. Jack Rogers and I have shared openly the genuine power of love. Jack is Chief Development Officer at the prep school in Philadelphia I attended for six years. The

William Penn Charter School. This experience has guided much of my life. Shaped my character.

Jack Rogers embodies all that the school is about. Reading this book captured my attention. Took me to a feeling that deepened me. Curious, in a way. But real. Very different. I write this piece primarily for myself in the hope I can sustain this feeling. Or at least return to it. Recapture it. Frequently. "The Power of Love" is a series of sermons and reflections shared by the presiding bishop of the Episcopal Church, Michael Curry. What struck me so hard? Like the mystery of faith itself? Curry repeats a constant refrain. Simply, "Hold on... hold on." He mentioned this four times in a chapter entitled, "Living the Way of Love." Living, "holding on"... to love.

Amidst it all. What's the answer? Curry emphatically declares... love is the answer. Available to all who will hear God's call. Give love. Receive love. Hmmm... Might be on to something here.

His words, my thoughts, took me further. I mentioned previously the decades-long Harvard study to define true happiness in life. The answer was just one word. "Relationships" Deep, meaningful, lasting relationships. As I digested this, I thought instantly about the thread through all the best, most nourishing relationships in my life. It was the power of love. Holding on to them.

Bishop Curry supports this premise eloquently here. During the sermon, he gave at the royal wedding of Prince Harry and Meghan Markle. He shared a story of this gathering of a group of young aspiring priests who were questioning their faith. Go get this book. "Hold on... hold on," he said. All I could think of. My grasp must remain firm. The possibility of losing my "hold" is always there. So, I must always "hold on... hold on."

Be steadfast. Not fall off course. Pray. Bless all you have. Be faithful to Jesus. Know him. Love Him. Love others. Love all. This flowed through my mind and spirit.

I'll read the rest of the book. The early messages were defining. "But Bob? Remember to reach out and thank Jack for the book. Hold on to his friendship."

# STRAP IN

*This celebrity really rang my bell one Sunday morning.*

Jon Batiste, the renowned jazz musician, once featured on the CBS show "Sunday Morning" told a spellbinding story. Surpassed only by the magic of his music.

He closed a twenty-minute interview simply by saying, *"Strap In."*

These two words beaconed the depth of his challenges despite his great fame. The emotional wounds he and his wife, Suleika, had experienced... are still experiencing today... somehow opened an intense feeling, a creativity and spirituality in them both. Driven by how Batiste and his wife (suffering cancer) had framed their lives. Centered their hearts. In positivity. Amidst the sadness. Sound a little "pollyannaish?" Well, this seemed to work for them.

Suleika, battling cancer, ultimately celebrated her remission with Jon. The illness came raging back two years later. But they pushed forward. No victimization. No anger. Just courageously chose the silver lining amidst the pain and anguish, the fear of her disease.

I'll paraphrase, try to capture the spirit of the last minute or so of the "Sunday Morning" segment. As Batiste sat at a piano, he tried to recall, to retell the experience he and his wife had gone through. "Unexpectedly, we found gifts amidst the anguish. Somehow, I could channel my anxiety into my art. My music. This released a 'wellspring' of creativity in me. A depth of feeling I'd never embraced before."

Then Jon went to the piano and played a brief, magical melody that simply mesmerized the interviewer. Even through the TV... I could connect with Jon and the deep feeling. On Sunday evening at the Grammy Awards, he won the most revered honor given to a musician... "Album of the Year." Amazing.

Finally, this, he shared...

"The anxieties and the joys. We all receive plentiful servings of both. How we blend or separate them is choice. Suleika and I found the joys amidst our anxieties. Separated the two. Tried to absorb in our hearts... all the joys. Not denying the anguish. Just making a choice to live in joy."

"Regardless of what one does. There is only one choice... Prepare... pray and *"Strap In!"*

It's going to be quite a ride."

# LET'S TAKE A PAUSE...

Where are we at this point?

My book so far has been an attempt to approach the connections between us that link us together in so many varied, different ways.

The purpose of Chapter One... Preparation. I tried to stress the necessity of taking personal responsibility for YOU, yourself. Accept that most, if not all, that happens in your life can be traced back to YOU. I started here because when one grasps this concept, takes responsibility, much of what follows will make sense.

We then moved on to Chapter Two... Spirituality. Most of the pieces in this chapter take the concept of love and approach it from a variety of perspectives. Stories, experiences, and ways to access the essence of life. Can one focus too much on a single topic when writing a book? As I may do here? Well, yes. But in this case, I think I get a pass. Can you write too much about our CONNECTIONS with one another... the love we are called to share? Nope... Of course, a buddy of mine told me once when I shared this with him, "Bob, not exactly a guy thing."

# CHAPTER 3
# RELATIONSHIPS

# RELATIONSHIPS

Chapter Three... Relationships. A wonderful joining of concept and action. Making love kinetic. Activating it. Putting it into motion. All relationships require a bit, if only a modicum, of emotional risk, before they become real. See anecdotes... ways to bring love alive in your life. Try to "feel" each piece. Sure. Understand what's being said. But more importantly, check in with yourself and see how you feel while reading ...

Here we go...

# S Curve

*We cannot survive life without the power of human connection. Without relationships, how could we ever know feelings of love? Without relationships, we could not grow. Growth only takes place in a relationship with another person. Relationships. Let's go look deeper... Every relationship we have in life goes through a cycle. We have a relationship with our own selves that follows the same path. Goes through the same cycle. I've used this tool in my coaching practice for decades. I've always opened a new engagement with S Curve.*

## "S" Curves

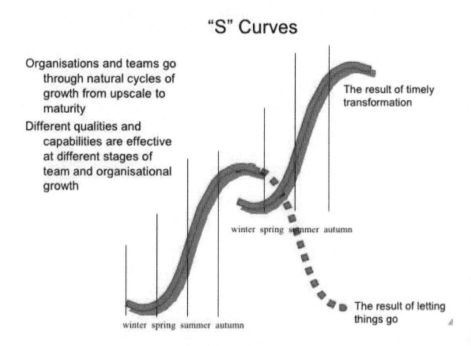

Organisations and teams go through natural cycles of growth from upscale to maturity

Different qualities and capabilities are effective at different stages of team and organisational growth

The result of timely transformation

winter spring summer autumn

The result of letting things go

winter spring summer autumn

We experience numerous cycles in our lives. We can't manage, change anything without first acknowledging it. Acknowledgment of the stage of life's path we're on is essential to navigating it successfully.

Picture each stage of the journey as an "S".

The cycle begins at the bottom loop of the S. This is where we prepare. Where we assess where we are. What is the right path? Its potential. How might we do traveling this route? What adjustments do I need to make before embarking? Like a pilot checking his plane, then adjusting his flight plan. If your assessments are on point... go!

Now, picture the more vertical section of the S. You've taken off. You're in motion. Energized as you travel the path you've set out on. Success is coming your way. Your plan is working. You are enjoying, reaping what you've sown. If you're running a business, profits are strong.

I'm rarely called to offer my consulting services when one is on this more vertical section of the S. This is what I refer to as "the harvest." Just pulling fish in the boat... hand over fist.

This brings me to the third section of the S. The top loop. As humans, we only have so much emotional and mental capacity. Only so much financial capital. We can only harvest, run hard for so long. Then we slow. Our efforts are yielding fewer results even as we strive to work harder. "What's going on?"

See the top of the S? It is the "plateau." We've reached the peak. Productivity and success may be at their height. But growth has slowed. Maybe to a halt. Time to coast? Or, as it's said, "Enjoy the fruits of your labors." Sure. But be careful. There's only one way to coast... that's downhill. The reality? As satisfying as being on a "plateau" can be? It's a problem if you try to stay there. Continuing to grow is the only option.

The question then becomes... what's next? The answer. Create a brand new S. And start anew.

If you look back on your life, your career, you will see it's been a succession of S Curves. A series of distinct cycles involving preparation, harvesting, slowing and ultimately plateauing. If you can assess where you are on the cycle, you will navigate your path more successfully. Those most successful that I've worked with will sense they are approaching a plateau and begin preparing for the next S early. They rarely get stuck on the top of a plateau. They just keep growing. Moving from one S to another.

When you step back, try to determine which phase of the S Curve cycle you might be on. This will help you plan, respond, and do so much better.

# Relationships...
# Make Us Happy

*I was intrigued by the following piece, citing the multiple benefits of healthy, nourishing relationships. Validated by none other than a professor who conducted a study at Harvard University. Get this...*

Yesterday, I read an eighty-year study at Harvard on "happiness." Involved seven hundred plus men and women. What makes one happy? Riches... accomplishments... pride... status. All the things we strive for?

Are these really key to what makes us truly happy? Don't think so. Not totally. According to Harvard... nourishing, lasting relationships. The health of our relationships fuels "Happiness" in life. Such was the conclusion of eighty years of Harvard research.

Made me think about my relationships. They exist at different levels. Social. Business. Family. The Harvard study I mention led me to focus on my more intimate relationships. Those special people in my life... those I cherish most. How do they impact me?

First, I've noticed a common trait that surfaces when I "connect" with one special person. My eyes moisten. Light up when they enter a room. A feeling of joy comes over me. By just being with them. Flowing conversation. Loving eye contact. A calming voice. Always some laughter. Serious stuff. Nothing stuff. A blend. I always come away with a sense of fulfillment. Wanting more of them. Those watering eyes of mine may be the most telling. "I am so fortunate to be with them always."

The Harvard study went much further in its study of the value of lasting relationships. There was the physiology. How nourishing relationships promotes good health. The impact they have on our psyche, our composure, our brain function... even our physical appearance. In essence, the study boldly posited that relationships are key to longevity. Youth. Memory. Alertness. Eighty years of research. Wow! Seven hundred participants. Seems like a credible study to me.

The people conducting the research admitted they expected a much more thorough, complex "Harvard-like" result from the work. After all, this was Harvard. Surely, the conclusions had to be more sophisticated. Maybe a large bound report. Not the case. Healthy, lasting relationships were the keys to happiness in life.

Again, to my amazement. One thought said it all. Beautifully. The key ingredient in living happily through life?... lasting relationships.

So, are some of the God-given blessings in our lives actually this straightforward? Right before our eyes? So simple. Our connections with one another can simply, elegantly, define a happy life.

I asked my coach years ago after our first decade together, "What's the purpose of all we've done here over the years? Where are we going?"

"Bob, all we ever do in our work together is... arm and arm... move closer and closer to 'love.' With pinpoint accuracy, he had defined it for me. The ultimate purpose of life. Reach for, move toward... Love. Simply... beautifully. And one of those irreplaceable vehicles needed to get there? Lasting relationships.

Happiness... Success... Moving toward Love. So clear. So revealing.

Thank you, Harvard.

# LAUGHTER...
# THE BEST MEDICINE

*I want to visit the one thing that speeds the fun of relating to another...
laughter.*

You get out of bed... you brush your teeth... you eat your breakfast...
you go to work... you come home... you eat dinner... you go to bed. Then
you do it... all over again. Or at least you used to. Remember that TV
Ad? All the things we do... almost unconsciously every day. Even amid a

PANDEMIC! In the throes of a devastating time... who knows how our lives will change? We don't. There are, however, habits... rituals actually (like those above) that remain regardless of where all this mess takes us. Phew! What a relief. Worst case? We'll all still be breathing!

But one thing not mentioned above? As important as our daily routines? The best medicine of all... Laughter. Yes. Laughter!

Sadness, anxiety, and stress are auto responses. They just are. They show up. Laughter, though, triggered by a joke, a video, or one of those hundreds of crazy, hilarious emails from friends. Such a relief. What a gift. Laughter is like a drug. An emotional escape from the hurt, the fears, the boredom. Laughter. The perfect, the best medicine. I have recently formed what I call my "comedic" board of directors. Three guys who drive me to hysteria... uncontrollable tears. Every time I connect with any of them. A great friend. An old fraternity brother. And my brother. Hilarity beyond control. "Did you hear the one about...?" "Go to YouTube and check this out."

Remember when...? OMG, the reaction... the tears... the "mini vacation" for me in the middle of it all. Johnny Carson... Jim Carey... Chris Farley... Groucho... and the incomparable... Don Rickles!... Jonathan Winters!... Milton Berle... Jack Benny... Forest Brooks... Rodney Dangerfield. Pick your favorite. I know. I'm dating myself here. More current masters of laughter? Seinfeld, Murphy, Rock, Gervais, Crystal. The above? Go there! Treasures All!

Laugh, Laugh! And laugh some more. Love who you are. Enjoy one of God's greatest gifts. The capacity to laugh. Just laugh. And then laugh some more... for yourself, for those in your "sphere" who look to you for confidence. Composure, fun, and laughter... they will love it. Laughter is infectious. A healthy sign. Reminder. We're going to be okay. Laugh and laugh some more. The best medicine of all...

# It's Not What's Wrong ... It's What Happened

*People I work with reach out to me... often lamenting, "Bob, what's wrong with me?" They want to know where their flaws come from. What are they connected to? For years my guidance has been...*
*"It's not what's wrong with you. It's what happened to you."*

"What's wrong with me?" This is the question my Coachies have often asked me over the years I've been coaching. "What's wrong with me?"... I have these issues I need to address. Why? Why me?" So, what's wrong? Really nothing. What you discover about you... the issues we all face are grounded in our life experiences. Who we are has evolved from... what happened... to each of us along the way. We are not grounded or defined by what we think is wrong with us!

Remember, though... what happened has added what's right in us, too. But it's human nature to focus more on our faults... isn't it? I've seen "a lot"... Alcoholism; obsessive-compulsive disorder; depression; poor self-image; marital strife. Other challenges. But to overcome difficult times in our lives, we all need to first have the confidence we can overcome them.

John is 58. He has lived most of his life avoiding failure, most everyday living with a need to survive. I've worked with him for years. Despite progress with behavioral change, improved health, he is still unsure of himself. Hesitant when making decisions. Unsteady about taking risks. Expressed to me often... "What's wrong with me?" "Why do I still feel this way?" I always replied, "Look how far you've come. The growth and progress you've made." To no avail. The hesitancy and uncertainty remained.

The key question that unlocked the answer? "Tell me openly, John... What happened? When you were young. When you were growing up?" We did a meditation. Discovered that he had suppressed an experience that was at the root of his lack of confidence. Actually uncovered something that happened to him when he was a young boy. Something he had suppressed. Had been there for decades. Lodged in his subconscious. He could not recall what had happened. That is... not until it surfaced during meditation.

John had struggled in his relationship with his father. Not particularly successful himself, John's dad had his own issues with self-confidence, self-worth. He pushed his son, John, hard. Expecting performance and behavior that set an incredibly high bar... The underlying message? My son will not turn out like me! John got excellent grades in school, but not straight "A"s. He started on the football team, but he wasn't the "star." John was a good, if not a perfect, kid.

This wasn't enough for his father. John had to be tamed. Driven to be more. "My son has problems that need fixing." So... what happened to John? His father sent him to another school. A school for problem children. At thirteen, he had to leave his good friends. Say goodbye to his first girlfriend... forced to attend what used to be called a reformatory... or "reform school"... a penal institution for troubled children.

The experience knocked him off his emotional bearings. Thrown in with teens with real problems. Anger, isolation, and confusion might best describe John's response to the experience. Why had his father dealt with him so harshly? Sent him to this subpar school. "Something must be wrong with me." No, John... this is what *happened* to you.

Thankfully, with work, John gained a new perspective. Grasped the reality that the experience differed greatly from his memory. If there was something wrong with John... the path forward would be much more intense. Much more complicated.

Happenings are much easier to deal with... even erase. But when he separated himself from what happened? Understood that what happened was not of his doing? John could embrace his new perspective. Nothing was wrong with him... it was what happened to him.

So, think about your own life experience. Insecurities, lack of confidence? What happened? Try to remember those experiences... that impacted you. Just know. There's so much right with you. Focus there. Happenings will matter less.

# Bars, Planes, and Barbershops...

*The people you meet and the books you read will shape you, your character, more than any other factors. I heard this when I was a young boy. Watched my dad connect with everybody. Didn't matter who they were. What their apparent stature was. Dad reached out. Whenever... wherever he was.*

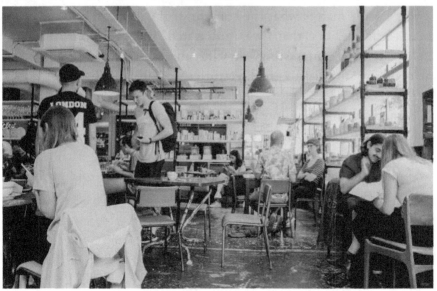

I decided a while back to act, to behave differently every time I sit at a bar, fly on a plane, or get my haircut. What do all these experiences have in common? The opportunity to connect with new people. Usually to my right. My left. People I have never met. Previously, I chose never to engage with them... any of them. Assuming a kind of "cigar store Indian" like posture. Motionless. Staring forward speechlessly. I now see bars, planes, and barber shops differently.

Those unknown to me were people who also stared, without speaking... just like me, as I had done for years. But a funny thing happens now. I choose to connect. Reach out lightly... test their willingness to chat. Maybe learn a little about those I had ignored in the past. "How are you this morning" I might ask. Never really knowing what response I would get. Some choose to "cigar store Indian" me. Sit there like a statue. A few, no reply. Game over.

But more often I would get a response to my question like, "Good, how are you?" An exchange would follow. Usually, about the frequency of visits to the bar, how often do you fly... what do you think is the wait time here at the barbershop? Most times, I would learn more about these unknowns. What they did for a living. What they thought of Atlanta or the airline? Or more simply, how their day was going. Didn't really matter what the content of the chat might be. The key was... I showed first that I was "interested" in them. I wasn't focused solely on being "interesting" myself... and bore my new acquaintance with all my stuff. Just a small gesture of kindness. Whether it be well received or not.

Sometimes this drives my family nuts. Reaching out, I mean. "There he goes again." But I'm so okay with that. Because I've met a select one or two people while doing this who have become friends. A few wanted a bit of coaching. Others (waiters, bartenders, and my barber) say, "Hi!" with a big smile and a hug. Just because I engaged with them differently than others might.

Ah! Case in point! I'm writing this on a plane. Early 7 am trip home. The flight attendant is delivering drinks and snacks. Maybe 120 passengers on the flight. I watch her coming down the aisle. I'm maybe passenger 50 to be served. As I gave her my drink choice. "Good morning!" she said with her Spanish accent, warm smile. She gave me my drink, for which I simply, so simply, said, *Thank you for your warm smile and energy this morning.*" She smiled even more brightly, put her hand on my shoulder, and said cheerfully, "Oh, thank you so much."

No big deal. Maybe my words made the remaining 70 passengers a bit more fun for her? Don't know. What I *do* know? Every encounter with another human being is an opportunity to reach out with a kind gesture or question. However insignificant it may seem. Again, not all will respond. Those who do are small little gifts. Gifts to myself.

So the next time you are in one of those situations where you and those nearby who sit, stand like "cigar store Indians"... remember. You never know what you'll get when you reach out to them. But there is no downside in doing so. A random act of kindness can go a long way.

# You Never Know Who's Swimming Naked... Until the Tide Goes Out

*A phrase I've used numerous times when deflection, confusion, untruths surface... during a coaching session. In a marriage, a business deal, with ourselves. The "blue dress"... Pete Rose... Hillary Clinton. Until you drain all the deception, fluff out, and get to real motives in the situation at hand... the "tide" will drown the truth. "You'll never know who's swimming naked until the tide goes out."*

We're only human. All flawed. I recently conducted individual coaching sessions with two wonderful people. Both open and honest. Making lots of money, have a great family. Both were confused, frustrated, (angry actually) about their circumstances. This person was doing this, that guy was doing this... "Can you believe I'm putting up with this stuff?!" Well yeah... you are! I listened intently to their lament, they were both playing victim here. "What if I told you that everything, everything you have shared with me here *is all about you*." Each gave me that familiar, incredulous look, *What do ya mean?*

Well, you never see your truth until you let "the tide go out." Remove all the cover, the empty, unnecessary chatter that goes nowhere. Your issues will be addressed when you accept your situation in truth. What you decide... how you will face reality. You're never going to change your circumstances. But you can change your perspective, your response to them. You can take responsibility.

The "tide" comes in. Covers our nakedness. Then the "tide" recedes. And there we are. Stripped of our cover. The truth surfaces. Left for all to see. Indeed we're naked when the "tide" goes out.

Years ago, I had a very toxic relationship with a business partner. He was driving me nuts. Controlling, dismissive of my opinions, his ego was off the chart. My stomach churned just being in a room with him. I complained, bit my fingernails. I was just so tired of it. The reality? This was all about me. My unwillingness, fear of letting the "tide go out." *Face the truth, Bob!* I told myself. I couldn't change my partner. But I could change my behavior. Change the painful dynamic between us. Get "naked" to the truth. This would not change until I changed. So, I took some time to think about how I would share my truth with him... as attractively, as eff ectively as possible. I did. After several long talks, I realized our partnership would not work. We split. The best outcome? Probably.

I had been wallowing in the water. The "tide" of hatred and angst washed over me. Pushing me away from the naked truth. To stop the madness, I had to let the "tide" out and deal with the reality of the situation. See nakedly what was before me.

Again, there are simply times we need to acknowledge that the truth will only be clear to *you* when you ger clear with *you*. You, your behavior, your decision to face your fears... bravely facing you. When you change you, watch your circumstance change in response. "You never know who's swimming naked until the tide goes out...."

# Δ TOPPER

*When we moved to Connecticut, we bought our dream home.*
*A realtor "friend" of ours came to visit one day.*
*"Oh, what a beautiful 'starter' home you have here."*

I thought, "Guess we better not unpack if our new home is only getting us started."

The other day I was telling another "friend" about a trip we'd just taken to see the Grand Canyon. Making little eye contact, my friend, without a comment or a question... immediately blithered, "Oh, let me tell you about my trip to Paris."

These are what I call "Toppers." You know... "I just love your new Honda! It even has some features I have on my Porsche." Essentially, those "Mine's bigger than yours." Moments that just want to make you puke.

But here's the trick. I've met with some of the greatest "bloviators" of all time. You know... big buck guys. Maybe a few homes here and there. A trophy wife on his arm. Sometimes a girlfriend on the other. Always lathered in excess. Cars, jewels, all kinds of "look at me" stuff.

Usually, the first time we meet? A tour of their home. Chatter about the stock market. Twenty minutes about their next trip. Or a recounting of their last one. About 45 minutes of, we'll?... I wouldn't exactly call this conversation, 95% of the talk being his. 5% mine. A relentless onslaught, gushing of "I'm better than yous" that will drown you if you let it.

But there's an antidote to either the brief topper, like "Paris." Or the version above. Simply give your "topping" friend no response, no reaction. Put a very subtle, disinterested, immutable smirk on your face. Try not to blink an eye. And above all... show no emotion. No "Wows"... no deep breaths. Absolutely no sign that what you are being told or what you're seeing makes any impression on you at all.

Let your egomaniacal friend burn himself out trying to impress you. Getting you to validate his existence. I've had to do this a lot. A bit passive-aggressive on my part, but such a relief, too. Slows the flow of BS. Allow me to take a breath or two as I lean against the tide of self-absorption.

Think I have an issue here? Of course, I do. But thanks for listening.

But maybe the response may help you someday when a "Topper" comes your way.

# Relationship...
# empty calories

*Relationships evolve on many concurrent levels.*
*The idea that "virtual" interaction can replace face-to-face...*
*presence-based relationship building... is fallacious.*

Zoom! "Why don't we just do a Zoom call?" Today? Maybe 3 or 4 times a day... I'm asked to have a Zoom call. With a coachie, a group, a friend for "cocktail hour." Hey! Now we don't have to drive anymore to see one another. Worry about reserving for lunch. "Is there room at the bar?"

Technology to the rescue! I may exaggerate here. But the chatter is that much of our world post-COVID-19 will be so great. Go virtual! Never did I think me in my underwear would be my new version of "biz" casual.

This Zoom concept is just one of those things that creep into our lives. It may not be as great as we think it is.

I've been concerned about younger generations today and their difficulty knowing how to truly feel. Really feel others. Empathy. Sadness. Feeling others. I ask my grandchildren now in their teens, "Are you going out with someone? Dating?" "No, we just 'hang out' in groups." Then I remember "puppy love." Those special few gals I dated in high school. Whether I ever got to second base or not. I had feelings for them. So old-fashioned?

It just seems the devices in our lives have made us more mechanical, more distant from one another. Yes? Back to Zoom. A byline in yesterday's paper. "Our world will never be the same after the pandemic. All those office buildings will be less full, maybe even empty. Businesses are running effectively. Our people are 'connected' virtually. Think of the savings. All the rent. All the furnishings. All of it!" Ok. On the surface? Logical. I need to get my work done on my "devices." Virtual business interaction has arrived. Big time! Is that person I'm talking to real? Or a robot?

Well... let's give this a little more thought.

This new way of connecting with one another may be what I call... "empty relationship calories."

Our relationships experienced on a computer screen. I get it. But it's not real. I can leave it. Go get my Coke Zero and turn it off whenever I please. Here's what I think are the potential gains and losses of going "virtual:"

### The Gains...
- Money savings
- Speed putting a "meeting" together.
- Showing up in pajamas, shorts ~... maybe even without either.
- Petting your dog while conferencing.
- Easier to take "breaks."
- Not having to suffer bad breath from the guy next to you.
- Checking your iPhone during meeting... undetected.
- Less chance those inter office romances will blossom.

## The Losses...

- Less Spontaneity, collaboration. Creativity.
- Not seeing the whole person. Their hand gestures, their warm smile.
- Casual interaction ... no office hopping.
- Less trust.
- Not fully feeling the energy (warm? cold?) of another.
- Observing how others handle interpersonal challenges. "Clean up your own lunch dishes, please!"
- Just lack of sharing person energy.

These are my pluses and minuses of Zooming. Come up with your own. It shouldn't surprise you if you've read any of my stuff that I am passionate about genuine connection. God's intended way that we should live with one another. How we feel in each other's presence, humanness. Virtual may be here to stay. But the next time you need to dispose of a dirty diaper after that Zoom, think how good that cluttered office at the old building looks now. Virtual may be the "in" thing. But my bet is like "empty calories" we may be consuming, eating the wrong foods? We may find lack of true human interaction while "virtual" may yield more empty relationships, too.

# How Lucky People Get Lucky...

*I love this one. Previously in "Bars, Planes and Barbershops" I talked about the value of taking emotional risks... reaching out to people you might normally ignore... pass by. Check this out. Some great examples... confirmation of the benefits of connecting.*

"He's so lucky. How does he do it?"

I listened to a TED Talk the other day. Given by a professor from Stanford University who teaches a course on, "How lucky people... get lucky."

She opened her talk with this story.

She was on a plane flight. Her normal routine? Earphones... immersed in her computer. But this time there was a distinguished-looking guy sitting next to her. To her own surprise, she uttered, "Hello"... her eyes connecting with his. A conversation ensued. Sixty days later? That guy sitting next to her on that plane published a book of hers that sold over 1,000,000 copies!

Seemed so simple? The word "Hello." But this is something so few of us take the initiative to experience. Appreciate. Taking the emotional risk of reaching out to others... strangers. Just to say, "Hello."

A young senior at my alma mater, Trinity College, was asked to speak at the commencement a few years ago. Not because he was the valedictorian. Not because he had even been a brilliant student. But because he had an important message to share. The title of his talk... "It all begins with... 'Hello!'"

Here's the essence of his speech... and I paraphrase.

"I was walking on the "Long Walk" (a stone walkway along Trinity's quadrangle) early one morning. A short African American woman approached as she was walking her small dog. I could have merely nodded. Casually whispered "Hi." Even kept my head down and simply passed her by. But as is my custom, I greeted her smiling with my usual volume and gusto... "Hello!"

She stopped. "Hello!" she replied. We talked. Nice day. What's your puppy's name? She asked me what year I was. Then I asked her, "Are you a professor here?" She replied, "Yes, I do teach. But I'm also the president of the college."

"The president of the college... Pass her by? And I'd never have known. Would have missed an opportunity. Since then, she and I have developed a great friendship. (While giving his speech, he waved and shouted 'Hello!' to his friend in the audience. She then waved and called back to him, 'Hello!')"

Moments where we all have all chosen to be open or be closed. A little relationship tension? Always. But just like the young man above... you never know who you might be interacting with or greeting with "Hello." I've made it a practice to remain open, to be aware of all those brief moments. At a bar... in the barbershop. Or while on a plane.

During a flight of mine recently, I sat across the aisle from a very large black man. He had headsets on, but I couldn't resist. Taking a risk, I nudged him and asked, "Who did you play for?" He smiled... "The Boston Red Sox."

He was Lee Smith. Fireballing relief pitcher, inducted into The Baseball Hall of Fame in 2018. A long conversation followed.

What was your best pitch? Who was the toughest hitter you faced in your career? What was the toughest thing about baseball for you?

Fascinating. Lee was so open. So energized by my reaching out to him. Two hours flying, talking, sharing stories. As we landed, he and I were still engaged. Exchanged emails. No contact following the trip... but what fun this chance meeting had been for me! Him, too.

And it all began with "Hello"

Why are some people so lucky? Well, maybe they simply attract lucky things their way. Certainly, one way? By just reaching out to someone and simply saying... "Hello!" Try it.

# TRUTH AND CONFLICT

*Regardless of how fully you value and nurture your relationships, there will always be differences between you and people in your life. Especially those closest to you. It's been said, "The closer you get to someone, the more you see the warts." Conflict. Inevitable. Check this one. Hopefully, you will find it instructional...*

I had a revealing session with a coachie the other day. He was telling me how conscious he was about "telling the truth"... always.

"Always?" I asked. "Yes," he replied... "always."

I challenged him. "What if you have an intense difference, a conflict with someone? Do you always tell him (or her) how you really feel about the problem... them personally?"

"Well, no. That could be hurtful. Not do him or me any good at all."

"So, you don't tell the absolute truth every time, do you?"

These were two phrases that surfaced during our conversation. What I learned helped me revisit my own concept of truth. Understanding that "Truth" is one of my immovable core values. Especially when faced with conflict.

The first phrase is...

"Learn to tell the truth as attractively as possible."

This is more science than art. Specific tactics can work well here. First, relationships are dyadic. One-to-one. Addressing conflicts with a group or even two at once? Confusing. Won't work. Bound to fail.

True "truth-telling" with another requires:

· Self-control, emotional restraint.

· Choosing the best, the right words to get your message across.

. Tone... tone... tone will be far more important than the words themselves. A specific "energy" fuels, accompanies any verbal expression.

Lead with negative "energy?"

· Sharp disagreement? "I'm right, you're wrong!" Look out... no space, no buffer, no room for compromise?... you're screwed.

· Anger? Maybe the most common, damaging emotion failing to resolve conflict. Get mad? You lose. If so... nice goin'.

· Don't accuse. Finger pointing... searing eye contact? No. If you do? Have a nice day!

· Listening only to the words in your head. No room to hear, to consider others. Childish.

· Facial expression that beacons to your recipient that the fight is on? This ain't gonna be good.

On the other hand, lead with positive "energy"...

· Think, pause before you speak. "Space before your notes."

· Sit down rather than stand. Puts you both on equal ground.

· Breathe three breaths; relax your shoulders. Calms you.

· Rehearse what you will say. Test the words and tone in your voice. Use a mirror. If angry... blow it all out before your encounter.

· Time? Pick a good one, a quiet one is best. No kidding.

· Actions. Once you have both purged your issues. Conclude takeaways. Do some things to prevent a repeat.

. Then offer this... "I'm sorry. We need to talk."

. Take responsibility for your role in contributing to the differences between you. Not, "You do this!"... "You did that!" Rather use "I" vs "You."

Ha! Just such a wonderful lesson for ME here! I've probably messed up more occasions than most by NOT practicing what I preach!

*"Duty calls us to get things done... but it's love that allows us to get things done elegantly, beautifully."*

I had to read this several times to fully absorb it.

Viewing conflict... "elegantly?" "All the negatives above? And love?" Didn't get it.

Then I remembered I wrote this in an earlier post.

"If God is love. And God created us all. And God lives within all of us? Then, there is something, however hard to detect or love in everyone we encounter. Regardless of the circumstances we may face." So, find the goodness here. Regardless of how challenging it may be to do so.

Learning to tell the truth as attractively as possible? Can be handled more tactically. Via the actions I cited. Getting things done beautifully? Much more difficult. Your true attitude will be determinant of the outcome here.

A heartfelt belief of mine. Issues with another can be and must be resolved, so you can move on. Being vulnerable to make this work. Expands you... resulting in a true growth experience. Go for it!

# Your Core

These words from my long-time trainer...

*"Bob, most of training depends on a key element. Strengthening your core. Your core supports your posture, your back. Has a lot to do with your overall physical condition."*

As I look back on another year, one distinct thought keeps coming up. With all the events. All the turmoil. The chaos we've experienced in 2022. One thought.

*"Never stop being you... never stop being yourself. Never allow events or circumstances to separate you from your core values, your core beliefs, your aspirations for your future.* My coach always told me, "Hold your space."

I believe we live providential, predestined lives. Commonly said, "You are here for a purpose." Another might say it this way. "The purpose of life is to uncover who you really are." Find that which makes you who you are. It astounds me to see how vast numbers today have little sense of their God-given *core.* That part of you that is immutable. There is a centrality to living a life guided and strengthened, by knowing... who you really are. Who you are meant to be. Just like working out. Developing, maintaining a strong body *core* is a central part of physical strength? So too is focusing on those things... unseen. In your mind and spirit that make you who you are. Things that define your *core.*

The movement away from the societal *core* in our country has resulted from a gradual, inch-by-inch deterioration of values, laws, behaviors that have governed us, fed us for the almost eight decades I've been alive. And long before that. War, anger, lies, bitterness of heart. Disregard for human life. Pornography. I could go on. All these have become norms. Movement away from who God calls us to be is unmistakable. Too many of us think, well... *"That's just part of life. That's just the way it is."* Wrong. So wrong. What's happened? What's happening? Is there a path out of this mess?

Maybe, maybe not. Why?

remember when gas was $.29 a gallon. That's right kids... $.29. It crept up and up over time when eventually it hit a threshold. $1.00 a gallon! Everyone went nuts! Today if we can get gas for under $3.00, we're happy as pigs in slop. Think of water flowing down a mountain that comes to a boulder. It doesn't try to force its way through. Patiently, water waits until the level rises to the top of the rock... and then softly pours over the top and travels on. Real change on any level... whether it be good or bad, occurs gradually... almost imperceptibly. Sinisterly think of Hitler and his march to commit the horrific. Gradual. Evil crept in. Until it was too late.

These experiences inch along. One silent, small step at a time. Until the you know what "hits the fan!" "How'd this happen? How'd we get here?" We've ignored the essence, the existence of our God-given *core.* That part of us that He blessed us with. So, what's brought us to this precipice? There are experts who direct their intellect to the variety of "crises" we face today. Moral? Climate, political? Global? They have convincing theories on why we're here.

*But you can roll these all up in a ball and toss them aside. We are in the midst of one crisis and only one... that being our gradual slide as a society. We are in the midst of a spiritual crisis. We are leaving God behind. Absent a spiritual awakening? We're screwed.*

Which brings me to the "Queen." Someone who refused for seven decades to allow these so-called societal "norms" to move her from her *core*... which in her case was her religious faith. Queen Elizabeth II died in September. Revered and celebrated the world over through war, turmoil, family strife. She held fast. Her *core* was immovable. A couple of others come to mind. Muhammed Ali and Nelson Mandela. Both known worldwide. Revered. In the face of unimaginable societal pressures... they held fast to their beliefs and values. Both paid a heavy price by doing so. But all three icons were immovable. They refused to bend to the pressures of our modern world. They held their space.

And that $.29 gas analogy? A Pew Research study shows that today 64% of Americans identify themselves as Christians. In the '70s... that number was 90%. Do the math. That's an average of 0.5% a year. Inch by inch. Imperceptible but relentless.

What does this tell me personally? Simply, I choose to just live my life striving to find myself. Answer... "Who am I?" Sort through all the stuff thrown my way. Every day. Always holding on tight to my God-given *core*. Sure. Politics, gossip, "cocktail" talk are convenient, easy norms to slide into. None of these strengthen or contribute much of anything. Our more personal thoughts, challenges are harder to surface in conversation. But I always remember the substantive stuff that comes from human interaction to encourage my family to live a life grounded in truth. Be yourself. Strive to know better each day... who you are. Uncover the gifts bestowed upon you by God. You'll never do this perfectly.

But living with an ever-strengthening *core?* Watch what a difference it makes.

# The Value of Friends

*Never forget your friends.*

A newlywed young man was sitting on the porch on a humid day, sipping iced tea with his father.

As he talked about adult life, marriage, responsibilities, and obligations, the father thoughtfully stirred the ice cubes in his glass and cast a clear, sober look at his son. "Never forget your friends," he advised. "They will become more important as you get older. Regardless of how much you love your family and the children you have, you will always need friends. Remember to go out with them occasionally (if possible), but keep in contact with them somehow."

"What strange advice!" thought the young man. "I just entered the married world. I am an adult and surely my wife and the family we will start should be all I need to make sense of my life." Yet, he heeded the words of his father; kept in touch with his friends, and annually increased their number. Over the years, he realized his father knew what he was talking about.

Because time and nature carry out their designs and mysteries on a person, friends are the bulwarks of our life. After 70 years of life, here is what he, I and you will have learned:

Time passes... life goes on... children grow up. Children cease to be children and become independent. And to the parents, it breaks their hearts, but the children separate from the parents because they begin their own families. Jobs and careers come and go... illusions, desires, attraction, sex... weakens. People can't do what they did physically when they were young. Parents die but you move on... Colleagues forget the favors you did... The race to achieve slows. But, true friends are always there, no matter how long or how many miles away they are.

A friend is never more distant than the reach of a need, intervening in your favor, waiting for you with open arms, or blessing your life. When we started this adventure called LIFE, we did not know of the incredible joys or sorrows that were ahead. We did not know how much we would need from each other. Love your parents, take care of your children, but keep a group of good friends. Stay in touch with them. They are truly one of life's most precious gifts.

*(Authored by Harvey MacKay).*

I can get a little euphoric about the value of relationships. Overdo it, even. But one thing this "Zooming" phase driven by Covid has revealed. There is no substitute for personal, face-to-face interaction.

# The Bridge Builder

*I conclude this section on relationships with this brief piece on "Friendship."
The author here is unknown to me, but his message is not. In my mind,
whether it be a couple... a brother and sister, or, well... best friends.
Friendships may be the most resilient relationships of all. There has been so
much written that giving is receiving. Personally, I can't hear these messages
often enough. Enjoy this one.*

I have great admiration for those dedicated to helping others. Ultimately, intending to leave a legacy. I'm acquainted with many successful people who've earned a lot of money. God bless them. They've succeeded in their way. Importantly.

Accumulation of wealth is a good thing. "Giving $ back?"... even better. But obviously, we all have so much more than our material wealth to pass on. I've learned a lot over many years. Lived through what I call the "accumulation" phase. Made some money. Lost some money. Built a few businesses. Have an incredible family. Life coaching has been an indescribable blessing. The "accumulation" years? What do I mean?

Thoughts, ideas, learnings. Picking up a little wisdom along the way. I've "accumulated" a bunch of all this. Gifts really that have been birthed by life experience. I think of Lincoln, Ghandi... more currently, Stephen Covey. All legacy builders. Great "accumulators." Those who have left an indelible imprint on vast numbers of others left one on me.

I'm now in the "distributive" phase of my life. I think about the great leaders above and so many others who have lived in "distribution." Understood that the gifts bestowed upon them must be shared, "distributed" to others... memorialized. Taught... passed on... while helping others learn and grow. No greater calling in my mind. From "accumulation" to "distribution." So natural, if not always seen in this way. But realizing this has been my pathway to joy. My version of success.

*I used to close speeches with the following. I offer it here without comment. I couldn't make my message any clearer. How I feel about leaving a legacy. "The Bridge Builder." Enjoy.*

*An old man, going on an old highway*
*Came in the evening cold and gray*
*to a chasm, vast and deep and wide*
*Through which    as was flowing*
*the sullen tide.*
*The old man crossed in the twilight dim.*
*The sullen tide had no fear for him.*

*But he turned when safe on the other side,*
*And he built a bridge to span the tide,*
*"Old man," said a pilgrim near...*
*"You're wasting strength in building here.*
*Your journey will end with the ending day*
*You never again must pass this way*
*You crossed the chasm deep and wide*
*Why build you this bridge at the eventide?"*

*The builder lifted his old gray head,*
*"Good friend in the path I have come," he said,*
*"There follows after me today,*
*a youth whose feet must pass this way.*
*This chasm which has not been naught to me*
*To that fair-haired youth, may a pitfall be*
*He, too, must cross in the twilight dim,*
*Good friend, I'm building the bridge for him...."*

# CHAPTER 4
# PEOPLE

# PEOPLE

# BOBBY

*Here's a fun encounter with an Atlanta Braves star. Bobby Cox was both manager and general manager of the team for twenty-five years. Always wondered how he magically led Atlanta to 14. I repeat. 14 National League Championships. I got a glimpse of Bobby one day while strolling on the beach on Amelia Island, Florida...*

Bobby Cox... "Bobby" as he's known throughout all of Major League Baseball... was the legendary manager of the Atlanta Braves. For an astounding twenty-five years. Under his leadership, the Braves won fourteen consecutive National League Division championships. Bobby was known as the "players coach"... I've always wondered why... what that meant. Then one summer afternoon while on the beach at Amelia Island, I learned why. I was strolling casually along the water's edge when I looked over and saw a middle-aged couple sitting in beach chairs. "Oh my God! That's Bobby Cox...." Not wanting to be just another zealous fan reaching for his autograph, I "played possum." Turning my head slowly, I simply uttered, "Oh, hi Bobby. Nice day." To my surprise, he instantly sprung to his feet. No smug, soft wave of acknowledgment as he slumped in his chair... as I fully expected. He was immediately in front of me. Our eyes met.

Then this from him... "It is beautiful down here, isn't it... Who are you? Tell me about yourself." Huh? This was a guy people fawned over. His celebrity in the Atlanta community was unmatched. "Who are you? Tell me about you." Totally off guard, I choked out a few sentences about my family, career, our twenty-five years on Amelia. "Don't you just love daughters?" "Is your place on the beach?" "Business consulting? What kind?" You can always tell when someone is listening to you. Is truly interested, can't you?

There is an unmistakable exchange of energy when someone absorbs what another has to say. Versus that too-normal, feigned gaze. Fake sincerity... while thinking about the next meeting or what they're planning to say to you in response. Bobby could have just stood there waiting for me to pour on the praise, the adulation. But no. "Who are you? Tell me about you." Ah hah... it was then I realized how he led a major league franchise all those years. All those multi-million-dollar guys. All those egos. Bobby loved people. Bobby Cox was and will always be remembered and revered as the "Players Coach."

Bobby was always about and always did what was best for his players. Never himself. Oh, he also holds the record for the most ejections from a game in baseball history. Somehow, I think this was further evidence of how he always supported his team. Most of those ejections were probably intentional. Backing his players whenever he felt he was called to do so.

Bobby was first and always... about his players. An uncommon humility, wisdom about him I've not forgotten. Just his listening with interest. Questioning. Learning. Always looking to hear more about another vs.

focusing on himself. Just one more example of what builds character. How some special people separate themselves from the pack. Like Bobby Cox did. On that memorable summer day on Amelia Island...

# You Never Know

*There's the-age old question...*
*"If a tree falls in the forest and no one is around to hear it,*
*does it make a sound?"*

I was at the dentist last week. I've had the same hygienist for years. She's pretty and fun. Good at what she does. I asked her, "On a scale of 1-10, how are you doing?"... "Oh, about a 6 or 7." Felt a sense of sadness in her, but I didn't pursue this further. Then she said, "Mr. B? I have a note clipped inside my purse. You told me a couple of years ago, 'Life is like a movie playing before your eyes... and you get to write the script.' I read your note a few times every week. Thank you."

Whatever you choose to do during a day, morning, noon, or night. Whatever the time. You never know... the reach, the impact of your actions. Just little things you think about, talk about, and decide to do. Take for granted.

All these "feed" you. Like the food you eat. Your thoughts, your actions, the decisions you make determine the quality of a day. "How did your day go?" Such a common question we ask one another at day's end. What did we do with our day? How do I feel about the day past?

Truly, we do lots of things. To make a living. Please a boss. To tell ourselves that we matter. But the greatest satisfaction of all? Comes when we impact someone else. Without expectation of payback or return. The amazing thing about helping, impacting another? It is the greatest gift of all. A real purpose that our lives should honor and appreciate most.

Today, as a coach. As I look back on all those times, I've asked, "How'd my day go?" I've treasured my days most when coaching, helping someone grow. Helping them move beyond past hurts. Overcome their mental and spiritual obstacles. Interestingly, I've found I need not be formally engaged in coaching to impact another. Like my hygienist above? Opportunities abound to reach out to someone. Impact their day, if only in some small way.

For years I traveled the country giving speeches. I thought this was a good way to reach the largest number of people. Have the most impact. After all, my message was exceptional. Just ask me. Surely this would have a lasting effect on all my audiences. Well, nice try.

The reality? Ninety percent of my audiences forgot 90% of my message sixty seconds after they walked out of the room. Speaking was always an ego boost. But fulfill my life's mission to have an impact and help people grow? Well... no.

I now work with eight great, loving people dedicated to growing personally. Who can deeply engage in achieving their life's mission? Helping them, watching them awaken? This may happen during a long session. Or this can simply happen during a brief exchange or comment.

What's more... they share what they learn, what moves them to help, impact others. Share the learnings we've uncovered during our coaching process. On and on. A chain of relationships that extends growth and learning. Who knows how long the chain goes?

I've discovered when I coach one... more deeply? I impact ten others. Maybe hundreds. The chain of growth, knowledge sharing goes on and on. Those I encounter leave me and tell others. Children, friends, business colleagues. You never know who. And all those speeches? They pale by comparison to the eight I coach today.

So, you see? That brief exchange with my dental hygienist had more impact than any speech I'd ever delivered. It had truly changed her, hearing a message of mine. No grand stage. No applause at the end. Just one young woman who today is doing better because she carries a small note in her purse.

You never know...

# Jack Rogers

*I was privileged to attend one of the finest prep schools in the country...*
*The William Penn Charter School in Philadelphia.*
*My loyalty to the school is strong... really strong.*

Since graduating in 1963, I've traveled from Connecticut and Atlanta for many years to join in special events at the school. You know, reunions, an important football game or two. Others. There were some unique special occasions as well. One in particular. Visiting a critically ill, beloved teacher and coach at his retirement home in Lancaster, Pa.; Celebrating the life of a deceased Penn Charter graduate who literally single-handedly changed the city of Philadelphia; taking part in fund-raising efforts instrumental in fueling Penn Charter's growth. The school continues to flourish today.

I thought back this morning about these experiences. Realizing how many alumni have had their own fun times at PC as well. Was there a common "thread," an individual who was ever present at most of these events?

Of course! Who else? Jack Rogers, Head of Development at PC. Here you go...

The teacher above, Phil Maroney, lived in Lancaster, PA... an hour or more away from the school. Jack loaded and drove a bus, taking about ten of us to visit him at his bedside. Meant the world to our struggling friend... and also to his now widow. Jack organized it. Energized the event as only he can! He does this a lot. His job? No... simply his passion.

Then there was the celebration of the extraordinary life of our revered fellow alumnus, Dave Montgomery. Long-time president of the Philadelphia Phillies. We traveled to Citizen's Bank Park, home of the Phillies. Jack Rogers handled all the logistics for a group of us. We visited PC before attending Dave's funeral. Hats, food, students, and staff to make those of us attending feel special? You got it. Jack did this, too. That's who Jack is – always about you... the other guy. He's always first about you.

Like most... who do the most... Jack Rogers operates under the radar. Reaching out to this guy, that gal. His "touch" radiates so much of what Penn Charter is all about. His influence is significant. Irreplaceable really.

I asked him once, "Hey Jack, when will you retire?" He had so tirelessly led development at the school for decades. So successfully. A tough job. "Bricks, they won't let me go." Surprised? Not. In truth, PC is in Jack's DNA. And PC has been the beneficiary of his passion. Simply, Jack Rogers loves people and loves the school. The school? The alumni? We all love him back. Jack may not want me to share this. He goes to Mass every morning. "Starts my day on the right foot." Again, no surprise. Jack's faith is palpable whenever you're with him. Just never wears it on his sleeve.

We've become good buddies, Jack and I. Yesterday, he texted me saying he was mailing me yet another of the so many special things he's thought to send me over the years. A PC hat commemorating the life of our dear friend above, David Montgomery. Remarkable.

I love this guy. We all do. He calls me "Dr. Love" Why? For another time. Just know the next time I visit Penn Charter for a reunion, a game ... whatever, Jack Roger's smiling face will be there to greet me lovingly. His Faith onboard. There's just no one like him.

# 3%ɘR

*I've been fortunate to meet people who just have a little something extra about them. They have a quality I call "It." There's another way to describe this. I learned about an extra "3%"... those known as 3% ers. From a new friend then. A dear friend today.*

It's Thanksgiving. And this comes to mind?! Maddening sometimes. But, well. Here goes...

Am I crazy? Sure. I think we all are. It's just a matter of degree.

It's 4 am. I awoke this morning with new "messages." I get these most mornings. This morning? Something a great new friend laid on me yesterday.

"Bob, you're a '3%er'" Huh? Here's what hit me... here's what's stuck in my mind at 4 am.

The Holy Trinity... 3 little pigs... 3 feet in a yard... 313 (my sacred number)... physical/mental/spiritual... you're a "3%er!

Could go on, but I won't. She didn't say 1 or 4. She said 3%! The number 3. Surely something significant about it showing up... as it does for me, all the time!

I meet people, rarely, who have a third gear... another dimension that separates them from others. They just stand out. There may be three, maybe four like these currently in my life. 3%? Is that what my friend was alluding to? She's been a "3%er" for a long time.

Let me explain. The voice is a magical instrument. It can sing, scream, and express a wide range of emotions. Our eyes, ears, sense of touch. All these help us see, help us reach out, and feel others... a special added dimension that brings us all in tune. But only if they have "3%" stuff on board. Magic? Yeah... kinda.

"Bob, you're a '3%er.'" She meant I have an added dimension. But I've learned most people are two, mostly two-dimensional. Not a judgment or criticism. They just dwell primarily in two dimensions. The physical and the intellectual (mental.)

So many of these guys run circles around me physically, intellectually. I used to be very intimidated by those stronger, smarter... "better" than I was. But something mystical has surfaced in me over the years. An added 3rd dimension I've mentioned above. The ability to feel more deeply than most. Allows me to see things others don't. Feel things others don't... truly feel another in a way others don't. The word that comes close to describing this. Spiritual. But, in truth? It's more than that.

It's an unexplainable connection with someone that fuels me. I always leave... wanting more of them. My new friend... and me. We are connected in this way. We are fellow "3%ers"

Do you know what a metronome is? It's a rhythmic device used by musicians and psychologists that swings back and forth... back and forth.

It's used to set a rhythm, a cadence for a song, or a meditation. It's therapeutic. This is how I feel when I'm with another "3%er."

We go back and forth... back and forth as we talk. Sharing, listening. The conversation deepens gradually into a third dimension. No BS. Real stuff. Can get, usually is, emotional for me as my feelings always intensify.

A metaphysicist has coached me for twenty-three years. I've learned from him that we are all actually multi-dimensional. We live in the conscious, the subconscious, and ultimately our soul. We're much more than physical, intellectual. As the adage goes... we only use 10% of our human potential. This, I think, applies to our 3rd dimension too.

Thanks to my wonderful new friend. She's a "3%er" for sure! And for the inspiration to write this morning.

Hoping you fill your special day with lots of love and joy... and maybe a little "3%", too.

# CHRIS

*All of us have special people who've come into our lives and make all the difference. My coach inspired so many of my writings. I honor him here...*

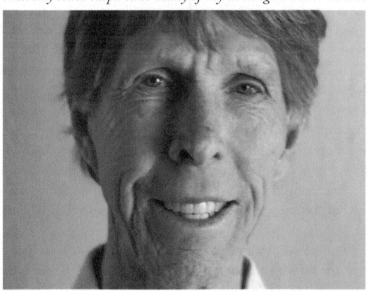

My greatest purpose here? Primarily to leave these writings for my precious grandchildren. But then my mentor, my guru called BS on me, *"Now Bob, you know why you write. You just love to write!"* He was correct... as usual.

Many times, when writing, I've referred to my coach. My friendship with him has inspired many of my writings. Twenty-three years. Just Chris Andersonn and me. Ninety minutes on the phone, every 10 days or so. He's in California. I'm in Atlanta. Only met him twice. First time? Five years into our friendship. Yep, five years before we actually met face-to-face. I'm an Episcopalian. He is a metaphysicist! "Really?" you say! "How does that work?" Well... obviously very well. No one does anything for twenty-three years that doesn't have lasting value.

Chris Andersonn is the most unique person I've ever known. Maybe because he is also the most loving people I've ever known. He began coaching me following my separation from the company I'd worked with for twenty years. I was so pissed off I couldn't breathe! Enter Chris. Enter a new beginning for me... at age 51. An age when my industry kinda saw me as, well, aged... too worn out to lead a team of people anymore. I'd done so successfully my whole business career. Then a chance call with a guy in California really... changed everything

What was next for me? What could a guy on the phone in California do for a devastated, martyred, washed-up exec like me? After all. Look what happened to me! Downsized, embarrassed, rejected. Woe was me. I was a victim of my circumstance. Right? Then this from Chris, "Bob, get over it... this is all about you." Me!? "What the hell do you mean? "Bob... Bob. It's always all about you... You create your own reality." This is where Chris and I began. This has been the thread, the essence of all we have done together for... 23 years. Creating my own reality.

The process with Chris engages a complex stream of thoughts, feelings, learnings I could not capture here if I tried. But by accepting that this works... has changed my life and led me to take responsibility. To become a true adult. Let me see if I can describe the relationship with Chris I've so loved.

He's a guide... not a professor or an authority. He's authentic. He's assertive, loaded with wisdom. But never in a judgmental way. He inspires confidence in me. He's patient. Good god... is he ever? Not a religious person in a formal sense. But deeply spiritual. Took a while for me to "get it." Still trying. But there's one thing Chris has taught me that stands above all. Everything in life that is fully experienced is first based on LOVE. Oh, by coincidence, I'm listening to "Wedding Song (There is Love)" by Peter, Paul and Mary. Just "coincidently" it shuffled up on my iPad. Just makes my point. Another CONNECTION. Our lives at the core are ultimately about love.

As Chris has reached out to me in love, I've learned to do so with others as well. Beginning first by learning to love myself. Then focusing on the goodness in others... however undetectable it may be. I've learned that feelings trump thoughts... always. Feelings give texture, color to thoughts. Makes me think about a musician vs a mathematician. The color, the magic of music. The precision, exactness of math. Feelings vs thoughts. Both are essential. Just different.

Chris told me a few years ago that I was a "map maker." Called to guide people to the growth and fulfillment they seek in life. But most find this so elusive. About my eleventh year with him... "Chris, how long are we going to do this?" Learned quickly from him that growth and love are infinite. "Oh, okay." "Listen to the 'whispers,'" he's told me. "Quiet yourself. Listen for the 'messages' from God, your other spiritual guides. They are there for you if you'll quiet yourself and 'reach' for them." I can confirm they exist. I receive their messages... those "fireflies" most mornings. Chris was right again... as usual.

I've only described a small part of what Chris has taught me. But what about you? Should you focus on your own growth? Find a guide like Chris? Give this some thought. Lastly, let me share with you what has fueled my twenty-three years with him more than anything else. Maybe this will urge you to find your own guide.

I've taken my learnings and passed them on to others. Whenever I can? They, in turn, have passed what I've learned on to others, and they on to others... and those to others. The reality. If I impacted one? It meant eventually I would impact hundreds... maybe thousands. For my Christian friends, a kind of "loaves and fishes" story. Chris and I will continue our journey together. Whether we actually talk. We are friends who have truly grown to love one another. Forever. I think I have helped him along the way, too. I've been so fortunate to help those I've had the privilege to coach. Help them navigate their life's map. Joining them, guiding them along the path they've chosen.

None of this would have ever happened without my time with Chris Andersonn. My loving coach, who helped me draw my own map and then guided me magically along my path to the fulfillment I enjoy today.

Thanks, Coach... With so much love, Bob

# MR. MCADOO

*Moments can shine, so we never forget them. He was with us for a long time. This was what I remember about a dear old friend, Mr. McAdoo, who recently passed away. A guy so special to so many for over 100 years. In February, he would celebrate his... you got it. His one hundredth birthday! I honor him here. For his life. A life so well lived.*

Always called you that. Never really knew you that well. But remember you so well. Dated Susan. Think you thought I was okay. You were hard to read. Stoic in a good way. Felt I made the cut, though. PC guy, athlete. You know. Some of the right stuff. Parents were good friends.

I remember your warm greeting... always. "Hello, Robert."

"What's Mr. McAdoo thinking?" usually popped into my mind when we met.

So many things I could share about you. But let me offer here my most distinctive memory.

Pace and Charlotte (my parents) both died at age 90. Their funerals took place at Laurel Hill Cemetery. Remember? You came to both services. Ambled in slowly, as always. You were early. The first to arrive... at both. I remember your gaze... one of a kind. Solemn and gracious. Always with that "soft" personality of yours.

As my family gathered for the ceremony, you approached us, looked each of us in the eye, and paid your respects. Individually. Thoughtfully. Respectfully. No receiving line for you... Mr. McAdoo. You showed up early... front and center. One-on-one, you reached out to each of us. Don't think you know how special, how appreciated this was. Thank you.

But this must be, in some ways, emblematic of your life. In the right place at the right time? With the right stuff? Without a lot of fanfare. Just with that knowing, confident way of yours. An instinct of what to do. Why, when, and how?

I know little about your career. Just that you were accomplished, and distinctive. Know that you can see the true quality of a man in the eyes of his children. Need I say more?

So on this day, your special, unique day... Happy Birthday!

Godspeed, Mr. McAdoo. Well done.

With love, Bob.

# OMAR

*He's unique. Simply one of a kind. I've known him for over twenty years.*
*Have sat in the first row watching him take on all comers while "in the*
*arena." He's invited me in. Into his life. His passions.*
*His intimate, so intimate love of his family. That's him below*
*w with his son, Omar Andres. Family will always be the center of who he is.*
*I admire this about him... above all else.*

But this is only the beginning of my knowing an expansive life lived with...
well, a boundaryless capacity to reach out to others... on so many levels.

Omar Haedo has been immensely "successful." You know. On a money, wealth dimension. This has given him the resources to serve his God in very special ways. Loving others. From a far-reaching ministry serving immigrants to consoling a young lady in distress needing emotional support. You will usually find my friend there. Present. All in, every time.

I don't pretend to know the full dimension of Omar's generosity. We talk every Wednesday morning. He normally opens with this, "Let's talk pictures." Omar's pictures reveal his values. His spirituality. His faith. Oh, he has a plane, a beautiful boat... plays the piano, too. But these take a back seat to his commitment to serve his God.

Okay... it's not all "sugar." Omar is sensitive, needy. Tells me this a lot, "Bob, they all want Omar." Sensitive, needy. Get it?

He's tough. There are few problems he won't take on. Requires intense effort. Omar tells me he is tired. Often. Because he leaves it all "on the field." Has got innumerable supporters. Some detractors, too. I always say there is a fine line between passion and anger with him. You want to know how Omar feels about something? Duck. His truth is coming your way. But he's always he's open to input. Always seeking ways to improve himself. He's a grower!

Be ready to defend your position when you engage with this guy. He's brilliant. Courageous. Says he sees "around corners." Means he's usually ahead of the crowd. Which he usually is. At age 56, he's on his fourth business. Omar doesn't build small. He only knows large. His fourth business is expansive.

His material success allows him to live high. Moved his family a number of years ago from his native Puerto Rico to Miami. Now get this. An example of his "boundary-lessness." High living? It's Wednesday. "Bob, I think I'm going to put the family on the plane Friday and fly to Atlanta for the weekend." Family knows. Their leader moves fast. Atlanta in 24 hours. Be ready.

I love Omar Haedo. Our weekly calls last about an hour. We could talk for three. I learn so much from him. Tell him so, even though technically I'm the "coach." Relationships are our primary focus. Omar is a mentor. Especially to his two boys. His employees. Really anyone who "wants

Omar." Thus, we share this. A passion for people. The Lord's work. Helping others.

Don't know how long our Wednesdays will last. We'll always be a part of one another, though. Moving together down our respective paths. Both dedicated to serving God's purpose. The true, unending connection between us.

# The Diet Coke

*I'm always amazed at how people come my way just by chance. The connection seems to be so random. But ends up being so meaningful. A simple chat over a Diet Coke. It evolved into a lot more. I now refer to it as... The Diet Coke.*

Something as simple as a Diet Coke. Sometimes that's all it takes. I actually prefer Coke Zero. But it was a Diet Coke... five years ago that led me to someone I wasn't seeking. Never really expected to meet. But I did.

All because of... the Diet Coke.

The occasion? An annual gathering of twenty fraternity brothers. This year in Wilmington, Delaware. We always focus the event on golf. Tennis is a "stepchild." Golf is king for three days. But one day, I had to pass on the golf because of a bad back. My friend, who wasn't a golfer, and not much of a tennis player, simply said, "How 'bout a Diet Coke?"

We had nothing better to do, so we sauntered over to the bar, pulled up two stools and began chatting. The usual stuff... "How's your back?" "This is a great place, isn't it?"

Then that question that is always so revealing? "How are you?" Ninety percent of the time? The answer is, "Great. I'm just great." But as the Persian mystic and poet Hafiz put it...

*"I have a thousand brilliant lies to the question, 'How are you?'... a thousand brilliant lies."*

Occasionally, when asked, "How are you?" one opens with his truth. Makes himself a little vulnerable. Shares something meaningful. Even though possibly cloaked, softened early on with a little humor.

My friend did just that. Feelings... failures... relationships... values. More. Oh, these certainly aren't the usual entry points of a conversation. You work to get to them incrementally if you get to them at all. Word by word. As trust builds. The two of you connect... one on one.

You see. My friend and I had graduated from college in the mid-sixties. There had been a forty-year gap between graduation and our meeting in Wilmington. We had known each other as students, frat brothers. Vaguely. That's all.

But, sitting on those stools, there was a nearly imperceptible chemistry between us. This fueled an early confidence in us both. We could "go there." Share openly, reciprocally. Tell all... without judgment. What had we done with ourselves over four decades? What had we learned? What had worked? What hadn't? Family, careers, desires... dreams.

You know when someone is truly listening... or not. Turns out we both had learned this art well. More interested in each other... than trying to be interesting to one another. With none of the usual "Mine's bigger than yours" stuff that we'd hear later from some of our other beloved fraternity brothers.

Two, maybe three hours later, we parted. But we knew we'd sparked a connection that would mean much to us both in the future.

There have been innumerable chat sessions since that first one perched on those two stools. Even one wonderful visit to his home in Annisquam,

Massachusetts. And a bonus... Our wives enjoy each other, too! Back and forth, my friend and I go. A love for one another that blends in more with each connection.

We will visit again soon. God willing. We will continue to play out this last quarter of our lives in style. We both have health issues. Neither life-threatening. But just present enough to make us appreciate one another... more vibrantly. As the journey continues.

Today? I buy lots of Coke Zero. But I always keep one Diet Coke in the fridge to remind me. Friends like George Bird are rare.

And to think... a relationship birthed by the Diet Coke.

# COΔCH

*This one speaks for itself...*

There's something about an occasional encounter with another that, well, how can I best put it... kind of touches your soul. Overly dramatic? Maybe a little. But such was the case when I met Paul Assaiante, legendary leader at my alma mater, Trinity College. Over ten years ago.

The occasion? A three-hour lunch here in Atlanta. Paul was a member of the Development staff. Was he cultivating me for a million-dollar gift? No. We mostly just talked about life. Good things... gratitude, generosity, character. Connected almost immediately on a spiritual level. Magic? Yes. Happens rarely with me. Happened that day. Thus, my desire to share this piece about my friend, Paul.

"Coach" Paul is iconic in the sports world for his almost mystical success with the collegiate squash program at Trinity. It's not my purpose to recount all of Paul's accomplishments here. Go Google "Assaiante" for these. Rather, I want to share a few things about Paul, the man that I remember beyond his extraordinary coaching career at Trinity.

First, the lunch. You know when an "energy" between two people unexplainably shows up. Such was the case ten years ago with us. Can't even remember the content of all we shared that day. Don't need to. Just recall vividly that it was special. Energetic, spiritual. Would put this guy prominently on my "map"... permanently.

Paul was in the midst of reaching heights as a leader in the sports world. But his emerging profile had little to do with our connection that day. We saw each other more as kindred souls, seeing life in very similar ways. Came away from my time with him knowing I'd met someone unique. We parted as we always do today... with an embrace.

Fast forward a few years later to an annual gathering here of the Trinity Club of Atlanta at the prestigious Piedmont Driving Club. Normally attended by twenty or thirty alumni, this meeting had attracted a packed ballroom of hundreds. "What's going on here?! Where did all these people come from?" Then from the corner of the room, "Hey, Bricks!" It was "Coach." He was speaking to the large group assembled. "Piedmont" has a serious commitment to squash. By now, Paul's legend in the sport was rising. Thus, the packed house to hear him speak. He was there to talk about squash. Squash and life. You could hear a pin drop as "Coach" took us through experiences he'd enjoyed with his kids. Who he was... What he taught... All he learned... Go read his book, "Run to the Roar" for a vibrant description of what I'm getting at here. Turns out Paul was a gifted speaker. His real gift? He always gave you so much more of his heart than he did of his head.

I've been a member of a group of twenty fraternity brothers who gather every year for friendship, golf... fun. Recently, we held our event in Portland, Maine. We needed a dinner speaker. "How 'bout the Coach! He'd be great!"

I called Paul. Remember his reply so clearly. *"Bricks, for you? Anything."*

Now, remember... I only see this guy maybe once a year. A call occasionally, about goings on at the College. But that's it. "Bricks, for you? Anything." That's simply who Paul Assaiante is.

Not the end of this story. Portland is a three-hour drive from Hartford. Did he make the trip to speak to us? Yep. Drove up and drove back... that night. Overwhelmed, I could not imagine, believe how much "anything" really meant! But that's simply who Paul is.

One last thing. A moment I'll not forget. I remind Coach of it often. During our evening with him in Maine, someone asked, "Coach, are you going to write another book?" With all the acclaim and renown. Seventeen national squash titles... here's what he said:

"Guys, my next book will be about 'Love.'" Love? Yes, love. He elaborated (I paraphrase here)... "All the wins, all the kids who have come through the program. Success was as much about love... love for the sport, for one another. A commitment and dedication that can only truly exist through the love in us all."

A book about "Love." The second he uttered the words, remembrance of our lunch years ago came to me. Our time together that day had been about love. Unspoken... both of us unaware. I keep buggin' him... "When you gonna write the book, Coach?"

They inducted Paul Assaiante into the College Squash Hall of Fame last week. I'll join the throngs who celebrate the numbers. The 252 consecutive winning squash matches... an NCAA record. All the other hard-to-imagine stats. But far more, I'll remember meeting a lifelong friend one special day who helped me learn something beyond winning in life.

In the end... whatever it is. Love will be at the center of our relationship. Thanks, my dear friend, Paul... so well done.

# MONTY

*This person's life lived might have influenced me
more than any I've ever known.*

I hope you have a friend or two you see infrequently, but always reconnect with instantly. A connection rich in history, that's emotionally resonant. Dave Montgomery was this kind of friend to me. Monty died. I'll not try to address his incredible resume here. Rather, I'd like to share a few stories, as many others will, about a guy, my friend who truly knew how to love. And receive so much more in return.

I approached Monty in 1971, hoping he would join my firm to sell life insurance. After imploring him to do so, he casually but sensitively said, "Bobby, I'm going to work with the Phillies." I replied, "Oh, as an exec trainee? In management? "After all, Monty has an MBA from Wharton... "No, I'm going to work in the ticket office." Wow... I'd lost out to a job pushing tickets through a window. Then this... "But if I wasn't joining the Phillies, Bobby, I'd accept your offer. You see, my dad died when I was a young boy. He had a $5,000 life insurance policy. The proceeds paid my way to Penn Charter (the prep school we both attended). The experience that changed my life." An experience that birthed a storied career in baseball with the Philadelphia Phillies. From ticket sales to Chairman of the Board. Oh... he did buy an insurance policy from me. At my 50th Penn Charter reunion in 2013, forty-two years later, Monty showed up. Holding that old insurance policy high, smiling broadly. "Bobby, I've still got it!" Forty-two years later. Tradition, loyalty. Call it what you will. I was touched. Monty had the gift of touching so many.

I never forgot how enamored, smitten David was with Lynn Sagendorph. A beautiful gal, that maybe Monty felt was just a little beyond his reach. Shared his feelings with me. Think many of us have had loves like Lynnie. Ultimately, she married a fellow Penn Charter guy. Had two kids. Game over for Monty? Not quite. Lynnie's marriage failed. Monty and Lynnie later married. Storybook stuff. A love that lasted until his passing. Magical.

Then, there was Bill Schweitzer. The counsel to Major League Baseball. A fraternity brother of mine at Trinity College. "Schweitz" knew Monty from baseball negotiations. Had immense respect for him and often told me so. When Bud Selig, then Commissioner of Baseball retired, Bill told me, "Bricks, if Dave wants to be the next Commissioner of MLB, he'll get the votes." But Monty turned it down. "I'm not very good at politics. Love my interaction with the players and fans of Philadelphia. That's me." So typical of him.

I was blessed to be with Monty the summer before he passed. Played golf with him at his club, Philadelphia Cricket. He showed up with a patch over his right eye. A cancer that had plagued him in recent years had returned. Affecting his optic nerve. "Bobby, without the patch, I see three balls." We played 18. Monty had 6s... 12s. One par. Recorded every score. Finished every hole. In the cart on #8... "Bobby, I've had a great life." Tears welled in my eyes. He knew his time was precious. We came to the 18th green. Monty was 45 ft from the hole. On the back fringe. Severe downhill putt. No way to sink it. Just keep it on the green! Bam! In the cup it went. That smile... the high five! Our eye contact with one another. What a final memory for me!

We will remember Dave Montgomery as one of the nicest people one could ever know. But you don't lead a baseball team to two World Series, and be revered as he was, without a lot of guts and determination. Monty had to make tough decisions. Cut this guy, fire this employee. In short... Monty was above all known to be nice, humble. But he could always "steel up" when his values came into play. You never questioned his integrity or his commitment to doing the right thing. Finally, the greatest lesson I take away from this life so well lived - his capacity to love others. Love all. Softly, humbly. Even a little selfishly. Huh? Yes, selfishly. Unique people like Monty learn early in life that true joy comes from reaching out in love to others and getting so much more for yourself in return.

Godspeed, dear friend. I just raised my arms one more time. In celebration. The indelible image in my mind of that amazing putt on #18!

# Events and People...
# Pass

*Infrequently, I will recall memories of those who had an impact on my life... who have passed away. My older brother, a best friend. My high school football coach. I'm always struck that each time I do, my emotions rise to the surface. Are so ever-present. Thus this next piece...*

*Events and People... Pass, but the emotions never die.*

THE WORLD SERIES has come to Atlanta!! I was watching the recap of the Braves' stunning third win last night over the Houston Astros. Peering through bleary eyes... after another third exhausting midnight TV vigil. During post-game interviews... "I remember..." was the constant refrain as reporters asked the Braves heroes to answer the age-old question, "How does all this make you feel?"

Get this.

*"I remember playing in my backyard when I was seven years old. Pretending I hit a home run to win the World Series."* Dansby Swanson said this. He's 26. *"I remember my mom telling me how much she hoped I'd be in baseball someday."* Brian Snitker is 66.

The events pass... but the emotions never die. Simply? We remember. I write here about connections. Those things we manifest through our emotions. Spirit that always touches us so. In 1980, the Philadelphia Phillies won the World Series. Game six. I'm in the box right next to the Phillies dugout. As I stood there? Wow... the energized crowd was intense. It felt like someone had plugged an electrical cord into my forehead. Amazing. I've never forgotten that night. The electricity in the air then. Today I shared this experience with a few of my more rabid Braves fans. Brought 1980 all back to me. I was right there.

1980 was four decades ago. A loved one passes away. We grieve. Over time, the hurt softens. It's said we leave behind the memories of those who pass away. Eventually move on from them? No... we never leave them. Nor do they leave us. We feel the pain and process our emotions, then tuck them away in a special place in our hearts. Only to be summoned months, years later. More distant maybe. But they never die. We don't leave our loved ones. We lock them away. Only to unlock them, unexpectedly, when we choose to recall them. And then magically... experience and feel their presence all over again.

People pass... but the emotions when we recall them... never die.

What urged me to write early this morning? A song by the "Temptations." The hugely popular soul group in the late 60s and 70s. As I listened to "My Girl"... their signature song immediately connected and transported me back to my senior year in college, fifty-four years ago. To a concert in our college field house. The "Temps" performed that day. The crowd, the stage... the chills. I pictured these magical performers as they did their thing. A song attached to strong emotions suddenly so fresh, rushed inside me? Like I was right there... once again.

One gift God bestows upon all of us is the gift of memory, recall. In my thoughts here? A question I posed in an earlier post...

*Are we human beings living a spiritual life? Or are we spiritual beings living a human life?*

Something to ponder.

I marvel every time I see someone recalling an event, a loved one. Or even a special song. That takes them back... where time is no factor. And watch their emotions rise to the surface. Tears welling up as they do.

The events we experience, and the people we love... pass. But the emotions will never die.

# "WE ALL COMIN' HOME..."

*Sometimes the most powerful impact can result
from the simplest phrase or statement...*

Nancy and I watched a movie last night. "Same Kind of Different as Me." In it, a beautiful lady played by Renee Zellweger, a wealthy widow, experienced a saddening death after a long bout with cancer. Her befriending a Black, homeless person in a village of "upper class" residents was the focus of the movie. More to follow.

But first. I've had occasional sparks of thought in recent months about my mortality. Natural, I guess, being in my mid-seventies. You know. How do I view the life I have lived? I hope with good feelings. Looking over my shoulder at it all. Pretty good, actually.

But the close of the movie last evening truly spoke to me. Djimon Hounsou... the fabulous African-American actor so memorable for his role in Stephen Spielberg's "Amistad" played the homeless person mentioned above. He had compassionately been taken in by his now deceased friend. At her funeral, erect, imposing in stature. Eyes fired with grief as he remembered his wonderful friend above who, though suffering a painful death, she had shown him love and comfort when no other would. The family had asked him to deliver the eulogy honoring his deceased friend to the congregation of "privileged" townspeople in attendance. They were stunned he was called to do so.

During his emotional memorial honoring her, he simply said repeatedly, "We all comin' home.... "We all comin' home." While there was no indication of his spiritual beliefs, this simple phrase from one who had little material wealth courageously stood tall. He needed no riches. "We all comin' home." We are... We are all coming home. Regardless of status, material wealth BMbm... "We all comin' home."

Like you? I live in the comfort I've known here in Atlanta for the last thirty years. My birthplace, Philadelphia, for thirty-six. Loving family and friends have made my homes vibrant, special. But this "... comin' home" phrase? Evoked very different emotions and feelings in me. "We all..." Not some. All of us. We all... are someday... comin' home. White, black, brown. Christian, Hindu... atheistic. All. We belong to one another. We will all arrive and join together someday. "Home." Then, I wonder. How will I arrive? Sad? Thankful? Proud? Reflective? Fulfilled? I hope so.

Norman Lear, legendary TV producer was once asked, "Mr. Lear, what age do you feel you are?"

To which he replied, *"I always feel I'm the age of the person in front of me."* Wow! How beautiful. What a great way to live! Norman Lear knows his time here isn't his choice. He, like all of us, will eventually... be *("comin' home.)*

When I heard this, I thought... you know? I want to try to live this way, too. Gives me joy of the present. As I experience whoever is in front of me. Loving them always. Some fully so. Others less so. But always focused on trying to love the person, the situation in front of me. I try to see events and interactions during each day as small arrivals, small "coming homes." Conclusions, closings of conversations. So many observations. Learnings. Each in its own way a "... coming home" experience. Gifts while here. Each of them... leading me "home."

So, in this light, "We all comin' home," told me... we are being called "home." Now. While here today. Whatever your beliefs. "Home" will be there for all of us someday. But "... coming home" invites us to love the wonder and be confident that "Home" is now. Right here in front of us. We need to live life to the fullest. Without fear. With gusto. Today. As God intended it to be. Just as Dijimon Hounsou declared, eventually... "We all comin' home."

# BB

*People... very young or very old. You always learn from everyone you meet. I've been blessed to learn a lot from three "nonagenarians." Defined affectionately as those 90-99 in age. All three of these guys have been guides for me. Wisdom filled. Both highly accomplished in business and, most importantly, in the way they have lived their lives. One is no longer with us. BB died earlier this year. He was 94. Claude is still here. He's approaching age 95. Jerry, the third, is 91. I honor the three of them here as people who enriched my life, as they have countless others.*

*One of my dearest friends, a true mentor of mine, died recently. A kinder, more elegant man I've never known. I'm picturing him in my mind at this*

*very moment. Expressing how much he meant to me. "Unique." One word that describes BB best. How I will always remember him, and my immense love for him.*

I met him on an airplane in 1989 traveling to an industry convention. "Hi, I'm BB Brown. Where'd you get those glasses?" (They were metal... horn rim. So like BB to notice.) "Where're ya from?" (BB is always more interested in you than trying to be interesting himself). Turned out we were both in the life insurance business. We compared notes... acquaintances. Shared a warm exchange. As we deplaned. "Great talkin' to you, Bob. I'm going to go get a pair of those glasses. Thank you." I thought to myself, "What a pro, such a gracious guy" At the time I lived in Hartford, Connecticut. BB in Atlanta. Nice chat, but probably wouldn't see him again. Wrong. Six months later, I moved my family to Atlanta to revive a struggling business there.

That guy BB... I remembered our plane ride together. Once you meet BB, he's hard to forget. I think I'll reach out to him. I did. But uh oh! I was new to town. Sent there to build a struggling business. BB was going to be my primary competitor! And a formidable one at that. But I looked him up, anyway. When I found him, he was just as warm as I'd remembered him. And not surprisingly, there was now a modest, professional distance between us. After all, we would be doing business with a lot of the same people. He turned out to be a very tough competitor. My toughest.

I will never forget BB telling me about the time he went to his local pharmacy and asked the druggist to sell him 5,000 aspirin. The stunned druggist did just that. You see, one of BB's greatest strengths was his ingenuity. He divided all the aspirin into two pill packets and sent one to his current and potential clients with this message. *"The next time you run into a business problem that gives you a bad headache, don't take these... just call me!"* Brilliant. Fast forward. BB got some of the highest quality business in Atlanta. So did I. Turned out there was more than enough for both of us. He eventually retired. I moved on to become a consultant. Today at his age 91, me at 73. We have lunch together once a month or so.

But let me get to my main point here. BB told me once. "Bob, if you use the word 'unique'... understand you're describing something distinctive. Something that's simply one of a kind. Unlike anything else." At the time

I thought, "I'm sitting in front of someone who is unique... simply one of a kind."

You see... although BB was very accomplished, he never felt compelled to tell me so or how much. His accomplishments are legendary in Atlanta. BB was always humble and a wonderful listener. A historian... a talented storyteller. BB always looked for and saw the best in someone. And that gaze of his? The same one he first gave me thirty years ago on the plane ride. Projected wisdom, integrity, and compassion seldom found. Just a few of the things that made BB Brown one of a kind... unique. I am proud to call him my friend. And as for that professional distance?... gone. Lunch in a few weeks. Oh... and today? If you run into BB? Take a look at those beautiful horn-rimmed glasses.

# CLAUDE

*We played golf together for thirty years. He was my landlord when I moved to Atlanta in 1990. He did a lot for me. But mainly he became a role model. Someone I've tried to emulate for years.*

I was new to Atlanta... loved my golf, maybe the friendships the game gifted me above all. Then there was that day in the summer of 1990 when that Series 7 BMW roared up my driveway to take and introduce me to

Settindown Creek. One of the great marvels the game of golf provides. And there he was... handsome with that smile, those welcoming eyes. "Here, let me get your bag for you, Bob." Hmm... do I have to tip this guy?

In an instant, a magical friendship that has lasted 26 fun~ oh, so many fun-filled years began. You see... if you're fortunate enough to embrace a beloved friend like Claude, you're just blessed. Simple as that.

All the good times... some real tough ones, too. We were there for each other. Claude has been immensely successful. Lead an incredible team at Piedmont Center, one of Atlanta's premier office complexes. At the tender age of 89 today, (his Spirit going on 50 by the way) this guy keeps succeeding. A proposed hotel in Roswell... the first ever! Quality, all he ever stood for, ever accepted. At 85 years young, he once told me on the 16th fairway at Settindown, "Bobby, I'm about opportunity, always will be." He continues to prove it... till this day.

But as successful as Claude has been. The great leader he's been with all his opportunities? This has paled compared to his success as a husband, a father, a man, and as my friend. Why? Because Claude Petty has a gift. I have always seen him as one of my truest, best friends. When I'm with him, he makes me feel like I'm the only person in his life. I think I'm unique. But I am not. I am just one of the many he makes feel the same way... every day. Just like his idol... Arnold Palmer (BTW... amazing resemblance between the two). You with him, him with you. That's it... always so very special.

One story. It was my daughter Sam's wedding at Ansley Golf Club. Big group, but Claude wasn't sure he could make it... darn! Wouldn't be complete if my dear friend wasn't there. In truth, I wanted to show him off to my legion of friends and family who had traveled many miles to be part of our joyous day.

I was at a table in the far corner of the ballroom greeting guests, my back to the doorway... Nancy was with me. Then it hit me... "Nancy, Claude's here!" "What do you mean, Bob?" "He's here... I feel his presence, he's here." I turned around, and there he was. Dressed to the nines. Silver hair shining. Doing his thing. Shaking hands. Making people feel good. Strangers? Didn't matter. His gift. Remember?

You see... I didn't have to "see" Claude come through that doorway. I felt his energy. That bright "light" of his that just told me with my back to the door... Claude's here! His "light" shines today... brighter than ever. Beautiful confirmation of how connected Claude Petty and I were to one another.

Oh, so many more stories I could share. But let me conclude. Claude, the "Silver Cobra" (our affectionate handle for him) is simply one of a kind. Broke the mold. The wisdom, the stories, the fun we have shared over these many years, have been... will continue to be one of the great joys of my life. I love Claude Petty. Always will. We may move on from one another someday, but my love for the Cobra will endure. The emotions I experience when I recall my days with him will live on forever.

Oh, by the way, I tried to give him $20 that first day... he wouldn't accept it. Of course.

# JERRY

*We all call him "Mr. Trinity." Jerry Hansen is an impact guy. As you will see, his reach is extensive. His impact on hundreds is legendary at my alma mater... Trinity College in Hartford, Connecticut.*
*I honor him here...*

"It's about time!" We hear this a lot. But this phrase applies particularly well here. I just finished reading an article written in "The Trinity

Reporter," a publication put out by my alma mater, Trinity College. Wanted to catch the spirit... my emotions at this moment. The article honored a friend of mine for his lifetime of commitment to a cause, a place he has loved... for seventy of his more than ninety years on the planet. Trinity College in Hartford, Connecticut. And "It's about time!" Many of us ask, "Why am I here? What am I called to do... be in this life?" Those who find the answers to these questions live a life fulfilled. I think Jerry found his calling long ago when he found Trinity.

The article in "The Reporter" is long. Beautifully so... There is a lot to cover. Seven decades dedicated to a singular passion. Being the best, he can be... for others. I'll not attempt to review the highlights of the article here. I'll leave this to others. Let me just offer this. "Gerald J. Hansen '51 P'74', '84, '88, GP'12, '16, '20. What do all these dates mean? Jerry graduated in 1951. His three sons graduated in 1974, 1984, and 1988. Three of his grandchildren graduated from the college in 2012, 2016 and 2020. Others, too. Legacy? I'd challenge any college in America to duplicate this lineage... this record. Jerry has lived a unique life. A life of giving. Because most of all, well? He's a giver. Memories of my experiences with him are still so vivid.

I met him in 1967, having just graduated from Trinity. The occasion? An alumni gathering in Philadelphia at the Inn of the Four Falls. Jerry was then the current president of the Trinity Club of Philadelphia. An event well attended. Philadelphia has always been a "pipeline" for sending kids to Trinity. I could tell immediately that Jerry was a leader. A take-charge guy. Yeah, known to us all... for years he had led an effort to get Philadelphia kids to Trinity. Just look at all the graduates over the years from Philadelphia. Just one part of his legacy. Jerry has his "touch" on so many of them. I was one.

I've joined him many times in person or connected by phone, complaining about what's going on at the school. This and that. At the end of every conversation though... despite our differences with the college? We've ended with this... "You know, I don't think I've ever met a kid who graduated from Trinity who didn't love the school." Seven happy graduates in the Hansen family might be the best confirmation of this.

A point to be made here. If you were to ask Michael Jordan how he made all those spectacular moves on a basketball court? He'd reply, "I don't really know. I can't describe it. It's just there." Now, of course, I'm not saying Jerry is a Jordan. He was a pretty good athlete. But no. Here's my point:

I want to share two distinct memories of Jerry that brought the Jordan reference to mind...

First, Jerry does have a "Jordan-like" gift. I've watched him circulate through crowds of Trinity people over many years. Students, alumni, parents, faculty... anywhere Trinity conducts an event, Jerry always seems to be there. Here's the gift. He can share a smile or a word... even just a glance that connects him to those he touches... always helping them to see Trinity in the best light. "Mr. Trinity" just does his thing. If there is a thread, a memory that has prevailed over my sixty years affiliated with the school, it would be watching Jerry "just do his thing." If I were to ask him how he does this? Like Jordan, he'd reply, "I don't really know. I can't describe it. It's just there." Yes, just like Mike.

Second, I've been fortunate to know, meet some great people who I'll call "significant." CEOs... professional athletes... great friends. Their accomplishments, their fame has impressed me. How they're admired by others. But as one dedicated to the art of human dynamics... I've noticed a quality each of these successful people possesses. Each has an uncanny ability that regardless of the demands on their time or attention. When they are with you, with me? You feel like you are the only person in their life at that moment. They're always totally present for the person in front of them. They listen. Make you feel you matter. Jerry has this gift. Do I think I'm one of his best friends? No. Does he make me feel this way every time I'm with him? Absolutely. Once you've met Jerry, he's hard to forget.

So... two qualities of an old friend I had to write about this morning. In the shadow of a wonderful article recounting his extraordinary life. If you want to know something about Trinity? Make a connection? Get insight? Even a "nudge" to help a kid get into the school. Call Jerry Hansen. He'll get it done. Be hard to forget.

God Speed, Jerry... so well done.

# Peter

*All the people I've described in this chapter are connected to me in distinct ways. All of them are or were people with character. Upstanding always. Regardless of headwinds, setbacks, tragedies in their lives, they stood tall. Showed their mettle. The following illustrates traits in them. In anyone, really. That helped define why they were so admired.*

When I was young... I'd hear "He's my best friend." Think you've said the same before? Well, I did too. I was in my late thirties when I met Peter. He died from cancer seven years ago. I honor him here. Think he was my "best friend."

*"A day without laughter is a day lost."*

Is it possible to have tears of laughter and sadness at the same time? For sure... this morning, as I remember Peter Sturrock. One of the best friends one could ever have.

Today is the seventh anniversary of his death (?)... (Betsy, correct me if I'm wrong.) Years ago, there was a Harvard study. "The Secret to a Fulfilling Life." The conclusion? Healthy relationships. Peter could have saved those smart guys a lot of time. He always knew relationships with great friends trumped everything else.

If you're fortunate enough to have one or two people in your life you trust with all and love unconditionally... you're gifted.

Peter and I attended the same prep school, same college. Amazingly, we never met until I moved to Hartford in 1981. I loved Peter. He loved me. Simple as that. Peter was wise. He was sensitive, caring, and empathetic. A great listener. All the stuff that makes one a great friend. I was serious, a little stiff, and business-like. Peter was fun-filled. A great party guy. Hilarious! We complemented each other. Worked together as business partners. Peter was large. In physique, personality, and above all, in spirit. We even looked alike. One night, sitting next to one another at a bar, a guy across from us blurted out, "Hey, are you guys twins?"

Tragically, Peter died of cancer. At too early an age. Our friendship lives on in me. In all who knew him. The events, the people in our lives pass. But the emotions... never die. To this day, he remains in my spirit, my soul... just as he was when he was with us. Betsy and Sarah. Both his treasures. Friends, friends. Stan, Bruce, Danny, Steve (RIP), Bill, Arty, Mike, Brian, Merle, Jerry... I could go on. Peter's friendships defined who he was.

We'd play golf together, kinda. Racquetball, kinda. Picture two, not in good shape, 220+ pounders pirouetting on a racquetball court. Pretty sight? Not. Even used to draw a crowd to watch us. Didn't care. We were just having a ball.

Traveled a lot, too. Golf trips to some magical spots. Pebble Beach and Pine Valley were the two most memorable. St Maarten, Bermuda... other places with our families.

Had gestures, sounds we exchanged, only we understood, "Ehhhhhhhh!!" for one. Huh? People thought we were nuts. Because we were!

Trinity College. We both served in several leadership roles as alumni. Were both honored with Alumni Awards of Merit. Peter sang in his church choir, kinda. Served in leadership roles there, too. Was first a teacher. Coached the golf team. Not surprisingly, his team never won a match.

He loved food. Large guy, remember? You could find him often at "Max on Main" and "Peppercorns" both great Hartford restaurants. But maybe his favorite? "The Golden Lamb Buttery" in Brooklyn, Connecticut. From appetizers to after-dinner drinks. If you joined him, be prepared to go the distance.

One of my favorite memories? Our "seagull trips" to my place on Amelia Island. Our "Seagulls" were birthed by the book, "Jonathan Livingston Seagull" about a bird who flew to wondrous heights above the clouds, above all the other gulls to learn who he was. We would share our dreams, our desires, our wins, and our losses. Talked about everything. We trusted each other so. Lots of Dewars Scotch always "lubricated" our conversation... Intimately connected. Every time we left one another, "I love you, boy."

He's here with me right now. Tears, chuckles. He moves me to share this with you. On the anniversary of his death. If there's a Peter in your life who gives you joy, helps you learn who you are, you're blessed.

I was. I am. Loving relationships. The secret of a fulfilling life. Thanks, as always, to you Peter for yours.

# ACUNA

*Changing gears here as I honor the people... I've found impactful as I've lived my life. I know, have known most of those I write about here. But the following about Ron Acuna... dynamic star of the Atlanta Braves? He is the epitome of the theme of this book. CONNECTIONS. Include him among the greats. How he plays the game of baseball. But more importantly, how he energizes, electrifies thousands every time he takes the field or steps to the plate. Magical.*

He's 22. Doesn't speak English. Don't know how he did in school. No college for sure. But put him in a baseball uniform... release him to run around a baseball field? He's a Ferrari.

Ronald Acuna, Jr. is, well... just a phenom. Plays outfield for the Atlanta Braves. When he's in a game? Everything changes. How his teammates play. How the crowd responds. How opposing players' gazes turn fearful. He's explosive. He hits. He runs. He fields and throws a baseball. All with Hall of Fame agility. At age 22.

l believe in energy. If this was about electricity, Ron Acuna would be the electrical grid.

A funny story. I first saw him when he played with the Gwinnett Stripers. While watching the Braves AAA team here in Georgia. A rather uneventful game on a Saturday evening. A great friend, Doug, salivates when he sees kids playing stickball in an alley. He's a baseball aficionado. Stats, trips to spring training in Arizona. Get the picture? He convinced me to drive 40 minutes north of Atlanta to see the Stripers play. "Hey Doug, how 'bout we go to a nursery instead and watch plants grow?" That's how excited I was.

But our tickets were ultra first class. Doug's treat. $8 seats... a mac and cheese, deep fried chicken and grits buffet included in the price. Wow! Pepto-Bismol at the door as we left for our seats. Said all about this feast. And then, there we were. Right behind home plate watching the Stripers play... joined by all the other twenty-five other rabid fans there in the stands.

As the game started, he gracefully waltzed into the "on-deck circle." Smack dab in front of Doug and me. Blocking our view of home plate. Doug doesn't have a short fuse. I do. He cared little about our temporary inconvenience. I did.

"Hey, #13? Could you move over a step or two so I can see?" Remember. First class $8 seats. And that Mac and cheese? I was farting repeatedly, loudly as it all rose to the surface. Not feeling great. "Hey 13...!" Nothin'.

Either this guy was arrogant, unfeeling, or deaf. Didn't move a centimeter. One more time. "Hey!" If I'd had any balls... I'd have reached out and grabbed his belt. We were that close to this clown. Nothin' He wouldn't move.

"I'll tell 'em to fine you!" "You're gonna whiff, you bum!" Just impossible to get this guy's attention.

Then he strode to home plate. Whacked the first pitch. Wow! Made me feel guilty about my disrespectful behavior. What was that? A cherry bomb? Maybe a car wreck. No. Just Ron Acuna hitting a baseball. I'd never heard a sound like that as someone hit a baseball. Ever.

Chipper Jones, Braves legendary Hall of Famer, once watched (heard) Acuna in the cage taking batting practice before a game. "I closed my eyes and listened to the ball hit the bat. I'd never heard it before." The cherry bomb. A car wreck maybe.

All to say that Ronald Acuna is off and running. He went from the Stripers to the Braves in 2018, and today is one of the most exciting, dynamic players in all of baseball. When he's in the lineup, the Braves are a different team. He's the spark plug. Like the Ferrari, he runs the bases. That rocket arm. And that sound of his bat is worth the full price of the $100 first-class seat watching the Braves play. A bag of peanuts has replaced the mac 'n cheese. "Gas" from Gwinnett still onboard. But my view is unobstructed. Acuna is the star of the show.

There is only one sports figure I've ever run to watch swing on TV... Tiger Woods. For years, I have marveled at his gifted, rhythmic movements on the golf course. I now see the same magic whenever Acuna steps to the plate. Like Tiger, he just wows me.

Whenever I "pass gas" today, I revisit that night in Gwinnett. The buffet, the great seats. All the fun with "Dougie"... inside joke. That I could not move someone who is, or may become. No... will surely become one of the greatest athletes of our time.

# ΛL ELSTEIN

I'm at Hartford's Bradley Airport having just attended my 50th college reunion. A weekend full of faces known and unknown. "Who's that?" ... was a question I had to ask myself all weekend long. My class consisted of an incredibly accomplished, impressive group. Revealed in part by essays we all submitted prior to the event. Awards were given during a beautiful ceremony on the Trinity College quad. 'Neath the signature elms the college is known for. You would expect Ritz-like treatment from an institution now billed at $70,000 a yr. for incoming freshmen. Right?! But no. We stayed in our old freshman dorms. Just as stark today as the day I lived in them fifty-plus years ago.

50th Reunion awards were given out. From the guy who invented the lens in all our iPhones, to the guy who invented devices physicians employ to reach inside us today avoiding invasive surgeries. He had over 120 patents. To the Governor of Massachusetts. A very accomplished lady.

Then came an award given to an alumna whose six-year-old son was killed in the Sandy Hook School massacre five years ago. She took her tragedy and turned it into a gift. She formed a foundation in her little son, Ian's name. And then went out into the world and trained over 2,000,000 families in the art of avoiding gun violence aimed at children. I was stunned. Impressed by all three for sure ... but none as much as I was by the unforgettable mother whose foundation lives on in fond memory of her deceased child.

As impressive as these graduates who were honored were, nothing impacted me more than a brief conversation I had with one of my old classmates ... Al Elstein.

I kind of knew Al freshman year. A quiet, very slight little guy. As he told me at ra eunion, "I'm very Jewish"... whatever he meant by telling me that. All freshmen in my time were required to pass a swimming test. Two laps in the college pool. We all showed up for our test one morning... naked. No one ever thought we'd need a bathing suit for a winter class at college in Connecticut!

We arrived at the pool to face the challenge. No problem. My classmates that day were able two swim two laps easily. All aced the exam. All but Al Elstein. He couldn't swim. While we all completed the test in a minute or so, Al lowered himself gradually into the water. He rolled over, floating on his back, and began slowly paddling, meekly, working his way toward the far end of the pool. Must share this too. He seemed almost "Christlike" as he lay his arms stretched out on the surface of the water. There were the typical snickers from our group. One even labeled Al, "The Blade" describing his painful two-lap journey through the water... like a knife edging its way along the poolside.

It took Al fifteen minutes to travel the two laps. He faltered, sucked a little water into his lungs along the way and paused a few times. But he made it. "The Blade!" He did it!! All the others had left by the time Al reached the end of the pool. I decided to stay that day.

During our reunion, Al came up to me dressed in casual clothes. A baseball cap pulled down over his narrowed eyes. "Bob Brickley! Hi!" I immediately thought, "Who is this guy?" Then, "Oh my God ... it's the 'The Blade!'"

"Al, do you remember the pool freshmen year? (54 yrs ago!)?!" Al smiled, "Yeah, Bob I do. Freshmen year was a very difficult time for me. No real friends, scared that I would never fit in. Especially after my embarrassing swim test that day."

And then Al said this ...

"Bob, I'm so glad I got to see you here. For years I've wanted to tell you this. You were the only person who was nice to me that day in the pool. You encouraged me. You congratulated me. When others left the pool that day, you stayed and helped me out of the water. It meant a lot to me. So much. Thank you."

All the accomplishments my classmates celebrated during reunion weekend recessed to the back of my mind. Those thankful eyes of Al Epstein stood tall ... up front in my memory. "Hi, Bob!" I'll never forget Al's greeting. My clearest memory. Clearest takeaway from my 50th college reunion.

Lastly, you know? I can't fully remember being so nice to Al. But then I thought, I really hope that I was. Ah, I know I was. His heartfelt greeting yesterday told me so.

Thanks, Al, for making my 50th so extra special.

# A Special Relative

*No conversation about people would be complete without writing about a very special member of my family. Aunt Sis was in many ways the matriarch of the Ziesing family on my mom's side. Our entire family is blessed in that we have stayed connected over decades. We reside from Philadelphia to San Francisco, New Canaan to Burlington, Vermont...*
*somehow, we all get along so well. Enjoy one another when we're together.*
*Aunt Sis, as you'll read, had a lot to do with this...*

My Aunt Sis died recently. Sadness for sure. But at 90? Good for her. Wow! Did the memories flow as I talked on the phone... to my brother, my sister, my cousins. The word that springs to mind as I remember her is... "elegant." Was she ever! Never really knew her well, despite her memorable presence at all our family gatherings in Philadelphia.

Over decades. Aunt Sis was refined... always so gracious, so welcoming. I remember some challenges in-laws had marrying into the family on my mom's side... the Ziesing clan. I heard she did. Know my dad did. But I always saw my Aunt Sis as so together. Formal. Again, always elegant. Had to work through a hard life at times with my dear Uncle Bobby... my namesake, my godfather. He, like my mother, suffered for many years fighting alcoholism.

I'm sure she had other issues, too. Her kids, my five cousins, knew about them. But all I ever saw was her constancy. Her beauty. That "twinkle" in her eye. Her loyalty to family. All those Holiday celebrations. My sister's "coming out" party. She hosted them all. One funny. It was Christmas at her retirement home... maybe ten, fifteen years ago. We had traveled up to see family. I was sitting next to my aunt at dinner. Felt her listening, seemingly very interested in what I had to say. When I asked her to pass the salt? She simply replied, "Oh, it's about 6:30." Oopsy... it was then I realized my Aunt Sis had a bit of a hearing problem. No matter. Same wonderful smile. Same elegant touch. My aunt was the last living member of my mom and dad's generation. A generation not defined as much by the love they openly expressed toward one another. Just not done in those days. But more by loyalty and tradition.

Even though all twenty-four immediate members of our family scattered over the years... we've stuck together. Loving one another? We remain committed to, appreciative of what we all had... what it means to be part of the family. Rare for sure.

We all came together in Philadelphia soon... for probably one last time to celebrate my aunt's life. The hugs. The tears. And when eyes connected?

The memories rushed in. For all of us. All the loyalty... all the family history in which my Aunt Sis had such a large presence and part in. And yes, as I really rethink all the love we have had for each other, too... over all these years. Expressed in our own unique way.

Godspeed, Aunt Sis... we all love you so. Well done.

# THE "ZS"

No... I'm not referring to s... as in sleep. Rather, I'm remembering the gathering of dear relatives of mine. The Ziesing family I featured in another piece. I'll call them the "Zs." It was one Sunday in Doylestown, Pennsylvania. The occasion? The Easter Sunday christening of the latest addition to our clan, four-month-old Ezra Ziesing. The "Zs" traveled from San Francisco, Charlotte North Carolina, Atlanta, and Philadelphia. Hundreds of miles. To attend this truly joyous event.

You see. The "Zs" have been in my life for 74 years... all of them. Special occasions. Every Christmas. A deb party or two. So many other casual get-togethers. We lived on the Main Line of Philadelphia. Home of the "elite." At least that's how many living there felt and still feel about themselves. The "Zs" somehow avoided this sense of self-importance. Pretentiousness. Oh, my mom was a high-profile "Z"... among the most celebrated debutantes of her time. She was a beauty. All the "Zs" were equally original. From my grandparents, Henry, Sr. (Pop) and Mary Belle (MeMa), to their kids, all their grandchildren, great-grandchildren.

And most recently! Our first great, great-grandchild, Ezra! This family has held together for a very, very long, wonderful time. We've suffered tragedy. The death of my too-young brother, alcoholism declared, maybe undeclared, even an affair or two... A couple of divorces. Most of Mom's generation are now gone. One beautiful, so regal member was still with us. My Aunt Sis, who I honored in this book. She traveled to the christening in Doylestown.

It's a gift that I've been blessed to grow up with all of them. My godfather, Uncle Bobby, was a metallurgist... there were execs like Gil and Uncle Henry and my sister Christine. Entrepreneurs like cousin Jeffrey, cousin Todd, and baby Ezra's proud papa, Todd. Insurance pros like cousin Chandi. My cousin Petey, who at age —- (You're welcome, Petey) still recruits key people for businesses in San Francisco. On and on. It would take a full page to mention the others. But let me just say... all were and are varied, accomplished... and so interesting.

During a post-christening brunch in Doylestown, we journeyed back to the memories... those happy and those not so much. One? As my cousin Cindy gazed at me, "I can see 'Yad' in you." (Her dad, my Uncle Bobby) The resemblance. Other connections galore. Experiences we all had in common. Evoking such vibrant emotions. Just a great day.

As we all sat in the pews for the christening of baby Ezra, the church Rector offered a brief message to open the service that captured this all for me. Ezra, his father, and his beautiful, young mother, were in the front pew.

Then the rector said this...

*"As most of you know, this church burned to the ground 20 years ago. I have a copy of the program (holding it high) printed for the service the week after the fire. There's a quote on the front page from a little eight-year-old girl.*

*"The church didn't burn down yesterday, only the building did."*

*"That little girl... now 28... sits over there in the front pew. Lovingly holding her infant son as we christen him this morning."*

Standing ovation! Welled eyes throughout. Wow! One of those spontaneous, shared emotional experiences none of us "Zs" will ever forget. There were similar poignant exchanges... memories shared that Sunday. I'll remember them, too. But none was more stunning than the message the rector shared that day. Thanks for a great weekend, dear "Zs!" I am so grateful to have you all in my life.

A standing ovation for my loving Ziesing relatives!

# MOM

*To end this section honoring special people I've known... I'm offering a tribute to one, if not the most, remarkable people I've ever known. My mother. Here is a sharing of a personal lifetime of experiences. I know all of you can relate, too. The joys, the challenges. All the ups and downs of the gifts of your mom. Here's my tribute to mine.*

I watched a Netflix series this week. "Surviving Death" is a documentary questioning whether there is life after death. Is there a "different" consciousness, presence once we pass on? Pretty compelling evidence that, yes, there is. Made me "feel"... reach for the most important person in my life... she's no longer here. My mom.

Picture yours as I continue this...

My mother was beautiful. Her portrait hangs in our dining room. Retrieved by Nancy among things to be trashed by mom when she decluttered her home in Philadelphia years before she died. So like mom not to see her beauty in this elegant piece. Thankfully, Nancy saved it.

A Philadelphia society debutante, mom was feted in newspapers and magazines as the model of a rising socialite. On a sailboat, just strolling, or simply standing there. She was photographed. Some clippings were saved. As was always true, the celebrations... receptions for young ladies in Philly society "coming out" flourished. Lots of partying, all fueled with alcohol. Probably where Mom's drinking started. It lasted for forty years. The first forty of my life. Blurred my connection with her, fully knowing her. I would later understand why.

She married Pace, a handsome Penn graduate. Great athlete. But according to my grandparents, from the "other side of the tracks"... of "lesser stock." Dad went into the Navy. He was in the Philippines when my two-year-old brother, Ricky, tragically drowned in a pond on my grandparents' property. I was but a few months old when all this happened. Had mom taken her eye off him? Was she careless while enjoying a second afternoon cocktail? Who knows. Ricky had just crawled away. He was gone.

Took Dad a few days to return home. Obviously devastated. Don't think he ever learned what really happened. A void, a wound that would impact Mom and Dad's relationship... until they both left us. Both at age 90.

Ricky's death defined so much of my life that followed. I think my parent's grief made an imprint on me even at my tender age. My mother was reserved. Introverted. Elegant. One funny story. I remember driving with her in Wayne... our hometown. A dump truck passed us with three guys in the back, headed for work. All three looked at mom in the driver's seat and whistled energetically in unison. *"Mommy, what are those guys looking at?"* She proudly replied, *"They're looking at your mother!"*

Mom was a real babe.

What I remember most about my relationship with my mother was the unspoken love we shared. With tears in my eyes, I tell you... I've been blessed with many treasures in life, but my mother's love surpasses them all. My mom was authentic. Gracious. Intuitive. Usually impaired by her drinking, she was known as a "functional alcoholic." Open, direct to a fault sometimes. Led Dad to call her "Gracie." Named after the gifted, witty comedian, Gracie Allen. When Mom served as a "gray lady"... assistant at Bryn Mawr Hospital, she was in the delivery room as a newborn baby lay naked on its back on the delivery table. Mom blurted out, "Oh, how beautiful. Is it a boy or a girl?" Get it. "Gracie" was like Gracie Allen... a lot.

I will always cherish that laugh of hers. I'd work hard to make mom laugh. And I was so good at it. Imitating her favorite TV characters. Telling her stories about school. Trying to give her a little relief from the issues she and my dad had with each other. Their relationship always felt tumultuous. So, her laughing breathlessly brought out the best in her. Separated her from the memory of Ricky. Sadly, I don't think she ever fully grieved. Never really got over his death. Events pass, but the emotions never die.

She drank excessively for decades. Dad felt victimized. Criticized her constantly. Blamed his career setbacks on her drinking. Threatened to leave. But didn't. Lived on all the years as a martyr. Had anger issues that certainly preceded his marriage. These intensified over most of my childhood. As the oldest child, I became the "lightning rod", receiving much of Dad's lashing out. Mom tried to be the bridge between us. Helped minimize a lot of damage issues Dad and I had with one another. Her love for me was indescribable.

All this affected me mentally. I had very low self-esteem as a young boy. Had great difficulty concentrating on my studies in prep school. Made up for it by hitting the books really hard. Got good grades. Amidst the turmoil at home, I needed validation. "Stop fighting! Just love me, please." My mother knew this. And oh, was she there for me? This particular experience resonates, comes to me now.

There were a few times that looking back... I think I was clinically depressed. An injurious event involving Dad in my teens. A return from New York City shortly after college following an acutely damaging experience with a job. What I remember most wasn't the despair and hopelessness. No, I remember the loving touch, the caress of my mother's hand as she softened my sorrow. Mom and I never really touched a lot or hugged much. The distance caused by her illness with alcohol might have been the reason. So, her touch during my periods of deep sadness was a gift. So intensely felt. These were our most special moments together. Here is one poignant reflection of my loving relationship with her.

I left Wayne with Nancy and our two girls when I was thirty-six. Wouldn't return except for holidays or an occasional visit. Things seemed to have calmed at home. Mom and I would always retreat to the kitchen where I would recreate all those hilarious imitations, recall the stories that once again... made Mom laugh and laugh some more. Drove her to hysterics.

Mom lived on after dad died. She had crippling arthritis. Could see the pain in her eyes when I visited. But she never whimpered. Never complained. You see, all those forty years she drank were followed by the best example a mother could ever give a son. The strength to overcome her alcoholism. Following six weeks of rehab, she lived for the rest of her life... for thirty-two years... not drinking a drop. Amidst the difficulty, the distance between us, and the love we shared... my mom was the most courageous person I've ever known. Hospitalized for six weeks at age 58 to get the "cure", she read a page a day from the self-help book, "One Day at a Time"... and never looked back.

Incredible...

So... I felt called this morning after viewing the aforementioned Netflix series. I've been writing for two and a half hours. This has felt timeless. Even a little "out of body." As if my mom was sitting beside me as I recalled and wrote about our lives together. Listening to her laugh... feeling her touch.

Is there life after death? I don't know. What I do know is that when I write, I go to another place. When time disappears... I somehow leave where I am. Don't know where I go. I just go somewhere else. And feel my most special someone, my mother is somehow magically there to meet me. Writing this has been cathartic. Therapeutic.

To love and be loved by my mother. The greatest gift of them all.

# CHAPTER 5
# EXPERIENCES
# AND MORE

# EXPERIENCES AND MORE

The books we read... the people we meet... experiences. These in large part define our life story. I've seen a lot of all three. Some have been formative. Some tragic. Some joyful. And some just fun and funny.

He died a very happy man. Maybe one of the happiest ever. Maybe because he left this earth... with *Enough*.

I know you'll relate to some of these as we all have so much more in common than not. We all want to love and be loved. We all need to relate to others. Family, friends, colleagues at work. Just acquaintances, too.

I reflect here on experiences I've had that have directed my path in life more than I realized before writing the book.

# AND DID YOU GET ALL YOU WANTED FROM THIS LIFE... EVEN SO?

*Experiences drive much of the content of our lives. I begin this with a beautifully thoughtful quote from Robert Frost. As you read through the experiences to follow, I hope you'll relate to some of them.
That they will trigger remembrances of your own experiences.
But, I think this piece is a great way to start.*

*"And did you get all you wanted from this life... even so?"*

This beautiful quote from a poem by Robert Frost is so thought-provoking. The symmetry of the verse challenges you and comforts you at the same time. There are two distinct parts to the line of poetry. First, "And did you get all you wanted from this life?" The second? "... even so?"

I've spent some wonderful years accomplishing much. Much of what I've "wanted" to get... maybe less of what I needed to get.

*And did I get all I wanted from this life?* Maybe.

But Frost's insightful, final two words, *"even so."* are haunting in their simplicity. I've built a resume. "I did this, I did that." I've tried to live my life in full. My family is a great family. Built three businesses. Had the privilege of coaching, guiding others through their life's journey. Had an impact on many great people. Truly joyous. I can picture it all. Some of it vivid. Some of it too distant to fully recall. Memories and experiences are indeed a magical part of our journey. Nostalgia, visiting our pasts can be so helpful too. Nourishing. More so in my older years. Maybe I even got "all I wanted"

Certainly, a lot.

Then the words, *"even so."* The second part of the verse. The trials I've experienced to get there... to "get all I wanted from this life." The missteps along the way. The regrets. Some guilt too... still lingering inside me. From happiness to sadness and everywhere in between. My challenges remind me of prices paid to become who I've become. *"Get what I wanted."* Maybe. But without the challenges, we could never truly appreciate our accomplishments. Find genuine comfort in them.

As I shared before, "the deeper you've been, indeed... the higher you go." From great challenge to great comfort and appreciation. This could not be better stated than by Robert Frost here.

*"And did you get all you wanted in this life... even so?"* A great opportunity to revisit the experiences in your life and reflect. Especially during the holiday season, celebrating joy... a new year and its promise of renewal... "even so."

# The Distribution Phase

*I focus most of this section on experiences, and things I've learned. But I don't own them. All are on loan to me. So, while they are with me, I am meant to share them. I'll never own them. I'm called to distribute them? Their worth? I have no way of knowing. No matter. I'll take the risk of sharing them openly. But well worth the effort if just one or two "score" and have an impact on another. Here is the gift of your "Distribution Phase."*

In the introduction of this book, I mentioned "fireflies." Quiet messages I get early in the morning that spur me to write. This morning? The word "Distribution" came to me. Then the word "Rain." Huh? Took me a while to clear my eyes to focus on what these words meant. How they connected with one another. But I got it. Ha! Caught that "firefly!"

Here goes ...

Our journey through life sends us out to gather experiences we've enjoyed, learned from. Events, travels... raising a family. We move through the years accumulating knowledge. Mentally, spiritually. Fueled, kept alive by our memories. Ultimately, some of us move on later in life saying, "Okay. Had some fun. Earned some money. I did well. That's it. Look at all I've done. Let's just move on. I've produced a lot. It's now my turn. My time to consume." This is how a lot of us see our later years.

But then there are... well, let me call them the teachers. The "distributors." Those who see themselves called to do more than just let their later years drift by. They see that something larger than themselves directs them along a different path. Bestowed on them by gifts of learning, wisdom to be cherished. Above all... gifts to be shared. Distributed to others.

The picture I have looks like large *raindrops* falling from the sky, landing on the trees, all the flowers, and plants. Essential for them to live, grow and flourish. *Raindrops* falling to feed, to give color and vibrancy to life. A magical process only nature can create.

This is how I visualized this connection this morning. That "firefly" and *raindrops* falling from the clouds. Providing an irreplaceable gift to life on earth. The message I want to share is coming to me. Like *raindrops* falling from the sky, so, too, are the experiences and the learnings of our lives. All the wisdom one accumulates during a lifetime needs to be distributed, shared, fed to those coming behind us. Helping them grow from what we know. From what we've experienced in our lifetime. Falling like *raindrops* from the sky.

Some examples... helping another find a solution that worked. Help them deal successfully with a challenge in a relationship. Sharing a message from a great sermon at church. Guiding one through a loss processed well.

A great trip you experienced. A story that delivers clarity to confusion. A book you read. A passage you've selected and shared from the Bible. There are many more. But you get my point. We are here to pass these and more... on to others. Like *raindrops*!

I call this the "distribution" phase of life.

We all experience stress in our lives. "I'm stressed! Ugh! What a pain. Can't stand it!" Many years ago, I had lunch with a very learned friend. Told him how stressed I was. Work, family, everything. I was so frustrated.

He said to me, *"Bob, how do you move a gigantic mass?" I did not know. "Friction," was his answer. "Friction?" He continued. "Know there is a fine line between stress and 'constructive tension.' Without friction... nothing moves. No tension, no growth. Embrace the tension as constructive. It's there to help you grow. Not take you down. Put it in perspective."*

Wow! Not only have I stopped seeing myself as a victim of stress. Instead, I realized I could pass the concept of "constructive tension" on to countless others.

My friend had passed on, distributed this wonderful perspective to me. I have since passed it on... distributed it to others.

Last week Nancy and I went to see Chris Botti, a maestro on the trumpet, perform with the Atlanta Symphony Orchestra. I wasn't looking forward to it. We'd seen him six years ago. The first half-hour that night was captivating, but Chris on stage playing his trumpet lasted two hours. Too much of him for too long. Whew! At one point, I was thinking of sending out for a respirator. But last week turned out to be very different. He played his trumpet as wonderfully as before. But this time he stepped back after playing for a short time and welcomed four young, aspiring musicians to perform with him.

They were absolutely amazing! I watched Chris beaming as he moved to the rear of the stage. He moved from the limelight. He was distributing. Mentoring those following in his footsteps. So clear to me. I watched his smiling face while he stood at the rear of the stage.

I think Chris Botti was living in his distribution phase.

This entire book is about my own *"rain."* Attempting to distribute learnings and experiences to you and others in the hope that a shortcut or two, a piece of wisdom might hit you. Help you move a little further along your own path. I think of my five grandchildren. My two daughters. Those I've coached. Friends, too. Hope they read some of my writings. What about the material possessions I'll leave to my family? Oh, I have some I'll "distribute" to them, too, someday.

But my true gifts to them will be the learnings, the experiences, the wisdom. All the wisdom-filled stories that like *raindrops* falling from the sky, will hopefully feed them. Help them learn and grow. Flourish.

I'm still learning more today. Just more "rain" building in the clouds. Look forward to sharing them during my time left. You too? Why not? The Distribution Phase... a signature part of a life well lived.

# The "Kid"

*The quality or success of an experience is most times impacted by decisions we make along the way. Take this path or that. Go to this restaurant or that one. Decisions that usually define how an experience plays out. Here's a piece that addresses the value of our "gut." The role our instincts play in the decisions we make...*

Decisions. Those points in time that define how life goes. Truth? You are the product of the decisions you make. For sure. Rationalizing facts, weighing plusses, minuses. The intellectual necessities. Essential. I've spent a lifetime interviewing candidates for jobs, helping professionals navigate their careers, helping people work through crucial times in their lives.

195

My advice? You've weighed all the facts... talked to confidants, colleagues, family members. Good. Now! Sit back, maybe with a glass of wine. Along with a little soothing music. Relax and ask... "How do I feel in my 'gut'? Regarding the decision I'm about to make? What's my 'gut' instinct? How might I feel a day, a week later after I've made my decision."

Most decisions in my experience are as much matters of the "heart" as they are the "head." Some rely entirely on facts. Okay... I get that. But in my view, "heart" trumps "head" many times. What your 'gut' tells you is defining. Here's the best way for me to illustrate "gut" feeling for you. A story about a young boy... The Kid.

*The Kid was Columbia's third-string running back. On the bench, every game, his uniform clean. Back to his locker after each game... uniform clean. Simply, he never got to play.*

*Then it was the Princeton game for the Ivy League Championship. Both first and second-string running backs went down with injuries in the first quarter. Uh, oh. Sitting on the bench... there's the Kid. The coach reluctantly takes a deep breath. Looks over, "Okay, Kid, you're in." The Kid scores two touchdowns before halftime, and catches the winning pass with 40 seconds left in the game. Columbia beats Princeton 28 to 26.*

*The coach runs up, eyes wide. "Kid! If I'd known you could play like that, you'd have been starting day one!" The Kid, exhausted, looks up. "Coach, did you ever see me walking across the field arm and arm with my father after practice each day?" The Coach nods curiously. "Sure, many times."*

*"Well, coach, you see, for most of my life, my father was blind. Last week he died. And today was the first game he ever saw me play."*

Feel that? That's your heart speaking to you. Listen to your heart... when you make those key decisions. Always trust your "gut."

# Pitching

*Here's my own experience living like the "Kid."*

"You're going to be a pitcher." I can still remember those words. My father's words when I was age 7. Like most dads, whether he wanted to admit it or not, dad always had a latent desire to relive his early life, through his son... me. My dad was a pitcher at the University of Pennsylvania in the late '30s. From what I can remember, he was just okay. "Okay" was never really good enough for him in anything he did. Maybe "You're going to be a pitcher." would give him a chance do better than "okay"... the second time around. His son was going to be more than "okay."

So, we started in the driveway when I was seven. "Get your arm back!"... "Look at the target!"... "Follow through." His instruction was right on! *Heck, I just got up right now from my chair and tried to go through that pitching motion he taught me. Almost fell over!* I threw and threw to dad in the driveway. "Hit that outside corner... right here," he barked. As he positioned that tattered old catcher's mitt of his on his right knee.

I was the starting pitcher on my Little League team at age 8. Even at that young age, I could feel that winning each game depended a lot on me... how well I threw the ball. The pitcher put the game ball in play. Can remember the chatter of my teammates behind me. "Get it in there, Bobby boy."... "Throw strikes." If I didn't, we were in trouble.

Played Little League for the next five years. Ultimately, as an All-Star. Our league played an All-Star game one Saturday against Radnor, a neighboring league. Thought I was a hotshot at age 12. I'd mow these guys down. Our game was on the 4th of July. An unusually large crowd on hand. American flags everywhere. Red, white, and blue streamers draped over the fence bordering the field. First time I really felt that kind of electricity in the air at an athletic event.

So, this cocky little all-star took the mound. I'll never forget it. My nervousness drained me. Then this kid came to the plate. Didn't know his name. Just that he looked equally cocky as me when he came to bat. "Hit that outside corner" buzzed in my ear. I threw a fastball low on the outside corner. Could hear dad, "Good pitch, Bobby!" This guy crushed it! Man, did he ever. A rocket over second base. I never saw it until it hit the snow fence in deep right field. Wasn't a home run. But the force of the ball broke two slats in the fence and went right through. Cocky little Bobby stared through his little eyeglasses. Looked over surprisingly at dad. No one had ever hit him that hard.

We went on to win. But dad told me after the game to go over to that kid and let him know that hit of his was special. I did. In addition to the "outside corner" this was one of those great lessons dad taught me. Be a good sport.

I continued to play baseball. Pitched in high school and college. Even a short stint in the pros. But all this pitching planted something indelible that remains with me to this day. Any success or failure I had on the pitcher's mound was great preparation for life to follow. Cast into a leadership role when I pitched, my team depended on me. It's been estimated that pitching is responsible for as much as 80% of winning or losing a baseball game. The pitcher was out there. By himself. You had four infielders... three outfielders... a catcher. And one pitcher. I had to be the spark plug that set everything in motion.

What did I learn? What knowledge could I pass on to my children, my grandchildren? About the value of playing sports. Any sport.

Let me list my thoughts here: *You never win or lose... you only win or learn.*

You always learn more from your losses than you do from your wins. You'll feel the sadness of losing more deeply than the joy of winning. Those guys I've bonded with most closely were teammates on sports teams. "Success is never final... failure is never fatal." Being professional, and upstanding following a loss builds resilience and character that you will never forget. "Poise", composure, and self-assurance, especially when under pressure. Being a leader carries with it a necessary loneliness. Requires you to take the risk of losing while focusing on winning.

So, I thank my dad for introducing me to pitching. One of the best things he did that helped prepare me for life. As I write this, I'm sitting in Westchester Airport dealing with a four-hour delay on my flight this weekend back home. Oops! They just canceled the flight home. I'll be spending the night somewhere. I'll just work it out. My capacity for handling this situation without complaint can be attributed directly to the lessons I learned playing baseball... Pitching.

# No Words

*I love listening to friends tell me about trips, their families, important stuff they want to share. I get word pictures. Feelings as their words, filled with emotion, define our conversation. But then, there are those times when there is an exchange between us that no words can describe. Writing CONNECTIONS has revealed a fundamental truth. Trying to describe some of the most cherished realities in life? Many times... there are no words. Love, faith, "describe the feeling." What is spirituality? What is happiness? How 'bout that incredible stunt that magician just pulled off?*

No words.

Love may be the most challenging of these life realities to find words for. CONNECTIONS attempts to describe all the wordless magic, energy we experience in our lives. I've always marveled at how professional musicians, gifted performers, athletes... can rarely describe how they do what they do. Perform. Some talk about a trance-like state they enter when at the height of an epic performance. Others simply shake their head and exclaim, "I really don't know how I do it."

There are simply no words.

The same may be true of any extraordinary accomplishment or victory. How many times have we heard this? "I'm at a loss for words." Or "I'm speechless." In fact, if you're able to describe an experience, maybe it's not quite as special as one you can't describe.

One Sunday, I watched a show featuring Adele... the incredibly talented songstress. Besides her amazing musical performance, she interviewed with Oprah Winfrey between sets. Casual, relaxed. When Oprah tried to get her to describe how she does it. She had... no words. She just laughed.

Yesterday, I watched Brian Wilson... a flick honoring the fabulous songwriter, performer who created "The Beachboys." He was interviewed. Brian is 79. He has suffered from a rare form of schizophrenia for most of his adult life. The interviewer asked, "Brian, many of your peers call you a genius. Elton John, Bruce Springsteen. All say there will never be an artist as accomplished as you." Can you tell me how you do it?

"No"... he replied. Brian Wilson had no words.

When a friend lives through grief because of the death of a loved one, we are often advised to "Just be there." No words are necessary. Becoming a grandparent! I've described this as the most unexpected, joyous event in life. An incredible surprise! There are no words to describe the feeling.

So, the next time you make eye contact with another person, whether it be in amazement. In anger or with love. With empathy or with sympathy. Think about it. Think about the *connection* between the two of you at that moment. No words needed. No words apply.

There are times when there are simply... no words.

# LUBRICATION

*A wonderful, long-time friend visited us yesterday. A lot of history. So much in common. We've traveled with her and another couple for years. Our trips go so well. Laughs, memories, old "jabs" at one another. So much fun! I've thought... "Why?" What I've come up with? Lubrication.*
*Trust, sense of how to best navigate... experience joyfully what we share.*

As a Life Coach, I'm often asked, "Coaching. What's that mean? What do you do?" Frankly, I've always found it hard to describe. Less factual, more behavior and feelings based... life coaching is more art than science. It requires listening deeply. Trying to explore the parts of one's human psyche and emotions that might help to define the issues to be addressed. Who they are? Where are they at this moment? Material wealth and accomplishments are rewarding. But only when blended with a clear sense of one's values, constructive behaviors, and a positivity that "lubricates" daily function?

What do I mean by "lubrication?" How do you lubricate processes to deliver the desired results? For those I coach in the business world? The ROI, bottom line guys? It's all about the impact on the dollars. You know. Where are the strategies, the tactics, and what's the financial impact? I address these issues as requested. But until this guy or gal grasps the real reasons he or she has engaged me? To "lubricate" the process by which they operate? Execution of strategy will fall short of expectations.

Behavior changes, resolving conflicts, differences in how best to grow. Values, a timeline for getting things done. These align and "lubricate" the strategy, the tactics to follow. I want to make sure we don't get bogged down in the usual frustrations and obstacles involving relationships that block important changes.

Recently the gifted Atlanta Braves star, Ron Acuna was benched for not running out a hit on the base paths. Acuna is the Braves' leading performer. Pull him out of the game? With all those home runs, stolen bases? No way. But the manager, Brian Snitker, chose sound behavior, team values, and attitude over performance. He pulled Acuna out of the game. He served notice to Acuna and his teammates, "The name 'Atlanta' on the front of your Jersey is more important than your name on the back." Thus lubricating the system driving this exceptionally talented group of athletes.

Lubrication is the stuff that changes the nature of interaction. Sets a tone. The "vibe"... the "chemistry." Snitker took the opportunity with Ron Acuna to lubricate his team. Let them all know. We are a team. The sum of our parts. Lubricating them with a sense of value, and cooperation is key.

# Sports "Buzz"

*The Atlanta Braves Are World Series Champions! There may be no experience in my life that has birthed my belief in connections more than the explosive excitement of a sports championship in a major city. I've lived in three. Two had champion sports teams. Enjoy... Sports "Buzz"*

In 2017, the Atlanta Falcons suffered the worst defeat in Super Bowl history. In 2018, the Philadelphia Eagles won an epic Super Bowl. One of the greatest Super Bowl wins in NFL history. Two games. Two outcomes. Polar opposites of one another.

Now consider the fan bases in both Atlanta and Philadelphia.

One enjoyed a euphoric "buzz" all over the city, celebrating the Eagles' victory. The other suffered through a sad, grieving process as the Falcon's collapse set in. No "buzz." in Atlanta.

I walked the streets of both cities following both Philly's great wins and Atlanta's tragic loss. The energy, or lack thereof, was palpable in each case. Intense. A lack of smiles and direct eye contact in Philly. Part of Philadelphia's culture. I usually feel like a windowpane when in I'm there. After Super Bowl LII? Nothing but warmth. Smiles. Eye contact galore. A felt the real "buzz" I'm Philly.

Atlanta's culture? Normally, you can't pass someone on the sidewalk without a nod, a smile... a greeting. Following its catastrophic Super Bowl loss? Heads down, shaking "No..." Even a few, "Can you believe it!" Like a low-sounding, sorrowful hum. Flowing through the city like an invisible lava. No "buzz." in Atlanta.

The Falcons have never recovered from their loss. Their record over the last three years has been pathetic. Same players. Same coach. They've not been competitive. Some call this a Super Bowl "hangover." I agree. But here's what I'm getting to. There's more here.

Not only is the team suffering. The entire fan base, the city of Atlanta is right there, too. What's amazing to me is that... the fumes of the "hangover" still exist to this day. Four years later. The pall, the pessimism. The absence of "buzz" or enthusiasm remains.

I talk a lot about energy. Connections. No coincidences. Only energy connections. Trillions and trillions of them. Intersecting, intertwined around the globe invisibly. Every one of us transmits our own unique energy pattern. In most ways, we determine the nature of the "energy" we send out.

We've heard "the power of positive thinking... just "think positively." Then, of course, there's the power of prayer. Miracles abound as prayer saves lives... can make the sick well. There's Karma... we can "catch the spirit!"

Back to my Falcons. Until the lull in energy infecting the Atlanta team... the community, dissipates? And a renewed "buzz"... positive expectation returns? I don't think Atlanta is going to return to a championship sports event. We will continue to be plagued by a lack of "buzz."

Lastly, and maybe most defining of Sports "Buzz?" The experience, the record of the squash team at my alma mater Trinity College in Hartford, Connecticut. We won 252 consecutive intercollegiate squash matches. Won. Let me repeat... 252 consecutive intercollegiate squash matches... WON! An NCAA record. "Buzz" squared. Elevated the national reputation of this small New England college. All by itself. Impact? Attendance at the school. Alumni giving. School spirit. Trinity was on the map! "Buzz" in the absolute. Heads high. The intensity of the energy here? Sports "Buzz." Without peer.

The power of the human spirit, energy... whether it be for good or bad. Is undeniable. Maybe this is no more evident than when it comes to winning, losing in sports.

"Buzz" The presence of energy can determine outcomes.

Good luck, Falcons. Acknowledging the need for "buzz" to return in Atlanta may be the first step in regaining the strength needed to return to the Super Bowl. Have faith Atlanta. We're due for a championship event to ignite our great city again. See the "buzz" return!

# Litte League World Series

**LLWS** - It's a rare gift when you get an hour, even a day with your grandchildren. But when you have three days? Well... just a blast! A lot of magic has to follow, and it did. Such was the case this past weekend. At the Little League World Series in Williamsport, Pennsylvania. With my three 16-year-old grandsons and their dad.

But first... the people there. The place. Like you I've heard a lot about the "forgotten" people in our country. You know, all those hard-working, faith-filled, genuine... heart-of-America folks. Welcome to the LLWC! A true celebration of middle America. 450,000 plus visitors over a couple of high-energy weeks. All that's good about America, the world.

You see... the LLWS is an international celebration. Tee shirts (rarely saw a collar), no Gucci shoes... every make of sneaker you can think of. Strollers, smiles, thank yous, eye contact, courtesy. Just down-to-earth moms, dads, kids. In a small upstate town in Pennsylvania. Celebrating a national treasure birthed in 1947. Actually met an usher there who was attending his 58th Series! Perfect weather. Seventy percent chance of sunshine every day!

The last time I experienced a vibe like this was at Disney World! One big difference. The LLWS is free. No tickets to the games. No reserved seats. To watch 13,000 fans daily over four games navigate the majestic stadium? No arguments about seats. Nothing but smiles. Unique. When they could be scratching one another for a seat on the aisle.

I will never forget the guy who noticed the lace on my sneakers was untied. "Here, let me tie that for you!" A faint message came to me. Jesus washing feet. Just me. But there really was a reverence about this place. Hillary called them "deplorables." I met firefighters, plumbers, policemen. Italians, Japanese, Venezuelans... Mexicans, Koreans. The team from the Caribbean. All there cheering their boys on! Ten to twelve-year-olds (one girl!) playing for an international title. No politics... no missiles... no anger. Just good fun. Music. Wild energy! Moms, dads, brothers, sisters cheering their guys on. A thrill! A blast! From home runs to colorful uniforms, hats. Language barrier? None. The thread of it all? Healthy competition, sportsmanship, and character. All the magical stuff that makes America great...

Now on to my boys. Triplets! Their passion for all this was infectious. Rubbed off on me, of course. This was their third visit. They love baseball. Any statistic or player's name is on the tip of their tongue. Ralfie, Willy and Jack. Gifts themselves. Polite, fun... loving. Wanted me there. I knew why the second I entered the stadium. Won't ever forget Ralfie slapping my shoulder just before seeing the beautiful stadium. Embraced, nestled in a small valley. Lined by high, densely treed hills. Wow! There was a special spirit here. We prayed a little. Laughed a lot. Just hung out - the five of us. Dad Ralf kept us all together In his usual loving fashion. I have to say, I've ticked off many things on my "bucket" list over the years. But this was the first time I had an experience first... then added it to my "bucket" list after being there.

This was the LLWS. An education, an eye opener, a "bucket" lister. Three days with Jack and Ralfie and Willy... Dad. In upstate PA. Amongst a wonderful crowd of people. At the 2019 Little League World Series in Williamsport, Pennsylvania. Unforgettable. Perfect!

# Pine Valley 2017

*Staying with the sports theme. This is truly one of the great experiences that changed a lot for me. When you're in the presence of a person, place, or thing in life that is unique.*
*One of a kind. You grow. Just by being there.*

The term, "experience of a lifetime" may be overused when describing a trip, an event you don't forget. You know... just a great time. This week I had just a great time! An experience that will resonate with me... for a very long time.

Two great friends, Gary and Patrick. Gary one of my best buddies and Patrick, our young Pro at my club here in Atlanta. The occasion? A trek to experience the wonders of the #1 golf course in the world, Pine Valley in Clemendon, NJ. I'd been to PV a number of times previously. Prior to leaving this time, I told my friends our scores would be way down the list of memories they would take away from this adventure. A truer thing I've never said.

Here I go... bear with me. This will take a while. But I have to chronicle this... all I can recall. First, our hosts. Hugh. My special friend for over 50 years. A more gracious guy you will not find. More on him later. John. My dear friend (a character) and old fraternity brother who joined us on the second of our two days at PV. As I said, I've been to PV many times. Our two hosts were wonderful. The staff there? Todd, Matt, Al, Bill, Sly, George, on and on. The incredible team there who anticipated and met our every need. Guests have never been so cared for.

Hugh has allowed me to invite myself to PV for years. I always take two from home who haven't had the privilege of visiting this magical place. As we arrived at the clubhouse, a well-dressed young man, Matt greeted me with this. "Mr. Brickley... how have you enjoyed that purple quarter zip you bought last year?" Last year!? I'd visited PV last year. Matt remembered my purchase?! No way. No heads up, no notes. Just his greeting. Got it? The people at PV? Are unusual. I'd say the average tenure of team members? Maybe 20 years. One, Sly the bartender, 45. None we met under 15. A culture and precision of excellence that's not to be duplicated. All invested, to make our stay special. And they did. You had to be there. Here are some of the highlights:

Pine Valley is "A beast never tamed."

We played 36 holes over two days. I lost one ball. Average at home per 18? Four. The Course is tight... at the same time generous... mostly forest-lined. Water on many holes. If my caddie had snorkel gear, I'm sure he would have retrieved the one ball I lost in the lake on #14. I've been playing golf for 60 years. Our caddies Jim, Chris, John... "incredible." Just three more PV team members dedicated to delivering this experience. Our scores. Gary and I are maybe 15-18 handicaps. No need to go further regarding us. Gary played great on the second day. I had some great moments. Self-promo? I parred the 602-yard 15th hole... twice. Had an absolute ball. Patrick our young pro? Let me share this...

I have a line of friends in Atlanta who cry, "Take me, take me to Pine Valley" No... I invited Patrick this time. He played the second day from the back tees. A greater challenge in the game of golf you'll not find. Talent, courage, character must reside in those who play from back there. Patrick shot 76, the second time he'd seen the place. I knew my choosing him was so right. He confirmed this over and over. By his play, His graciousness. Back to our host, Hugh. A handsome, authentic guy. I've always marveled at his storytelling. But he's a very private person. Two martinis at dinner one night, however? Truth serum.

Get to PV and he might tell you one of his stories. Like being chosen to witness an emotional, tearing, Arnold Palmer one evening as he was informed by the club's President that he was being invited to become a member of Pine Valley. Yes... another "incredible." piece to savor. Maybe nothing more tells you what PV offers golfers. They come from all over the world to experience it.

There was the food. The precision of each service offering. The course attendants on the course all dressed in white overalls at 6am as they prepared, and manicured the track for the day's rounds. Hole 5 Par 3, the signature. 230 yards to a postage stamp green. It would take a separate piece to describe the 15 minutes the golfer spends on this monster. Depending on where you hit your tee shot. There was the simplicity of the clubhouse. The tiny sign on #1. "No mulligans!" All so understated, loaded with the history and lore of the place. Classy... so classy.

The other members we met enhanced the experience. John, a wildly expressive broker from Greenwich, CT with his entourage. So many others. This guy too. A bit of a blowhard. "Where are you from?"... "Boston, Cape Cod, and Florida." My reply. A bit sarcastic, "Is that all you got, Bill?" But this kind of self-promotion was rare. The class and substance of the guests were palpable.

But here's the bottom line. The primary reward that summed the trip up for me. What I will most remember from our two days. Patrick sent me this text the night we got home.

*"Mr. Brickley, thank you for such a wonderful experience that I will never forget and will cherish forever. For introducing me to such wonderful people. The stories Hugh shared with us were were absolutely amazing! Lost for words. This was simply life-altering."*

What can I say? Just can't wait to take my next two.

# WINNING AND YOU

*Regardless of how I may view Tiger Wood's failings, I cannot fathom his feat - winning his last Masters in 2019. I doubt there has ever been a more Herculean effort in the history of sports...*

This Tiger Woods story will be told for years to come. A legendary athletic feat that stunningly evolved before our eyes. Maybe unparalleled in all of sports. Tiger was old, by golf standards. Many of the experts considered him to be washed up. He'd never win again. He would only be playing in the 2019 Masters because he was a past champion, as all past winners did. Certainly, he didn't qualify to be there.

Not to overdramatize, but the dynamics of Tiger's actually winning the 2019 Masters extends beyond golf itself. Sunday's scene on the 18th green on that Sunday expanded my grasp of the capacity of the human spirit. Not to hyperbolize... and I'm not saying Woods even remotely resembles a saint. But I always marvel at how episodes in life like this year's Masters, carry with them, bring to mind "Christ-like" qualities we can marvel. Tiger did so for me. All the vilification... all the judgment Ultimately, the fall. Finally, the "resurrection." The glory of it all. Woods seemed to have experienced all the phases the greatest person on earth went through. Kinda. I hesitate here so as not to be called sacrilegious. But these common traits came to mind as I teared up last Sunday watching the emotional, so human, celebration by Tiger after winning this Masters golf tournament.

Indeed, there are many victories in sports and in life that evoke emotional responses. In sports? Muhammad Ali... Ben Hogan (Google him)... 1980's US Hockey team. In life? Abraham Lincoln... Nelson Mandela... Stephen Hawking (Google him, too). All men who achieve the unimaginable expand my comprehension of the power of the human spirit.

We often hear that one of the greatest things about America is that "You can become anything you set your mind to be." Never accept less than giving your best to whatever path you choose. Tiger Woods is just the latest example of the power in each of us. God-given, it's up to us individually to draw upon, and realize our potential. And in our own way, eventually celebrate our own wins, as Tiger and others I cite have done. Tell us we, too, can do unimaginable things. Win! As Tiger Woods showed at the 2019 Masters.

# Music

*Went to see "The Fab Four" at the Atlanta Symphony last night. Wow! Four incredible performers recreating the magical, images and music of the Beatles. They tour the world. No wonder. Their ability to imitate was hard to comprehend. A wondrous experience... Here's "Music."*

We know that music can ignite the emotions, and soothe the soul. From Streisand to Springfield. From Celine to Sinatra. Music has magic, doesn't it?

Music always plays when I write. Seems to "lubricate" my thoughts and feelings... my words. I'm writing right now. Music is playing. Music has a way of getting inside us. Deeply, for some. Less so for others.

I'll never forget seeing "The Jersey Boys" in New York (four more times after that); a concert given by "The Bee Gees" forty years ago in Philadelphia, tearfully listening to their perfect blend. Then there were "The Whiffenpoofs" (Google 'em) four years ago at Yale University. On and on. These musical moments still resonate inside me.

Think back. Remember when a musical, a musical moment, or concert touched you? Go pull up your favorite song. Just sit quietly. Close your eyes. Swoon or bounce to it. Let it move you... take you somewhere else. To that special place in your heart, you'll always have reserved for it. I'm listening now to Perry Como's "Ave Maria." One of the most beautiful songs I ever heard. Better than any calming medication for sure.

Music... if you listen to music continuously as I do? Note how most songs embrace themes of romance and love. That's what music does. It reaches out in love. It somehow softens the compressions of life. Just a bit. Can fuel you with spirit and energy for what's ahead.

OMG... go get Alan Jackson's "Remember When"... or an unforgettable trip through life. Sinatra's "It Was a Very Good Year"... Or the beckoning of Streisand's genius melody in "The Way We Were."

We can harken back to a song, a tune, a performance that still... rings your "chimes." Look at the facial expressions of those performing their music. A famous singer like Celine Dion. A maestro on the guitar like the late Glen Campbell. Or Itzhak Perlman on the violin. All magically immersed in their craft.

Music... I remember singing a soft tune, a nursery rhyme to my three-year-old daughter... now 47. Seeing that innocent, beautiful look on her face. Golden... as she listened intently. Her eyes without a blink. Only music could create a wondrous moment like this. I recall it with her often... share it with you here.

Music and its magic. Wondrous...

# COBBLESTONE
# ROMANCE

*Here's a cute little experience Nancy and I enjoyed and chuckle over as we recall our visit to Sicily in 2018.*

Italy... 2018. Check out these impassioned words of our exceptional guide, Mario Marcosano, as Nancy and I journeyed through southern Italy last week...

"Ladies and gentlemen. I couldn't help but notice Bob and Nancy holding hands yesterday as they walked along together on the cobblestone walk. So romantic. Such a beautiful, loving couple."

Well, we *do* love each other. Forty-seven years strong. At least one of us for sure is stunningly beautiful. But "romantic?"

Let's examine this hand-in-hand romance Mario alluded to a little more closely. The city of Palermo... Fact. Ruddy cobblestone streets cover most of Italy. Large cobblestones make walking extremely awkward, difficult.

"Bob and Nancy walking together holding hands. So romantic." Ok... The rest of the story? Nancy cries out, "Bob! Will you please slow down?! Grab my hand and hold me up, damn you! I'm going to fall on these stinkin' cobblestones!"

Don Juan? I was not. More like Nancy's human "walker" without wheels. Oh well, what might you expect after 47 years. Two cobblestone romantics. Propping each other up on the streets of Palermo, Italy. Hilarious! And romantic, after all.

# Four "Daze" on Harbour Island"

*Oh, this one was fun...*

A few weeks ago, I told a friend of mine I was taking my girls to Harbour Island. Our idyllic vacation spot in the Bahamas. Just the four of us. Most I'd told said, "Wow! That's amazing." I expected the same reaction from my friend. But he said, "Took my two kids and my wife to Switzerland skiing last Christmas. All the old family dynamics showed up." "Oh," I replied, "not us." Well, welcome to our first three "daze" on Harbour Island. Flight? Perfect. Welcome from Jen, the manager there, and her crew. Wonderful. "Goombay Smashes." Our greeting cocktails. Two of these and you are an AA candidate.

Daze Point #1. Daughter Lisa had called us from JFK before departure. Her hubby had been put on straight commission at his job. Stressed out, he wanted her to come home to him. No way... She arrived safely. Our vacation was underway. Okay. Dinner Saturday night at the hotel. Curried Mahi Mahi! How does chef Krishna do it? Got to bed early. We're here! Lisa cannot believe it.

Sunday morning. OMG! It's Darla (not her real name) Lisa's old friend from her prep school in Connecticut. She was on the Island! Wow! "Come see us!", Lisa cried. Darla did. Mistake. The conversation that ensued. Well, shall I just say it was "interesting"... actually more like an episode from "The Young and the Restless." New York style.

Daze Point #2... A bunch of divorced women were with Darla. On a huge yacht. One was on her fourth marriage... Now 42, she'd gotten married again this week to a 30-year-old. Women's husbands in and out of rehab. On and on. Get the picture? They'd all come down to party with the natives. Darla related all this to us like she was just brushing her teeth. "Just life in the big city," she said. Yeah, but of course! Hmm... doesn't look good.

The weather Sunday was a little rainy. So, to celebrate the Sabbath, we sat at the hotel bar and had a "few" cocktails. PopPop more than his share. Laughs, fun with the staff. You know. All the stuff that made our family experience at Harbor Island so special. So far, so good. Dinner at the "Rock House" Saturday night. Premier place among many on this tiny Island. Amazing!

Daze Point #3... Returning home, PopPop's foot slips and he falls on the walk into our hotel. Cracks his forehead open. The old Howard Cosell quote came to mind. "Down goes Frazier! Down goes Frazier!" Down went PopPop! All-day cocktails had nothing to do with it... Right! Bleeding like a guy dragged off "Hacksaw Ridge." "Dad... Dad." Sam and Lisa took charge! If I ever believed my precious daughters might not step up someday and take care of me in my old age. Erase that thought. They were amazing!

Jay, a great young man on the staff, held on to me like a vice, steadied me all the way as I stumbled to a golf cart.

Off to the "emergency room" down the street. Looked like a barracks at Fort Benning. But no, there's Margie, a little Asian nurse! Uh oh. "Kum in, Kum in. I call Dr. Farrington."

A stern-faced doctor Farington shows up minutes later... I'd awakened her. Oops. Not in a good mood at all. "Sir, at your age! Wun drink a day! Wun! That's it!" (She didn't buy my story about my foot slipping on the path.) Maybe my alcohol breath and crossed eyes tipped her off? PopPop got stitched up. Went home with his girls. No more Daze Points... Phew! I hope and pray! But recalled what my friend who went to Switzerland had told me. "Family dynamics" Good luck.

Daze Point #4... One thing we learned Saturday morning. Lisa's friend Darla hung out with a bunch of crazy, partying 40-year-olds. Wild... let's just say they were all "misbehavers." "Lisa, Sam... "Come out with us after dinner!" A party! They did. At a place called "Pink Sands." It was crazy, but the party was soon over. When leaving, there were fifty golf carts in the parking lot all lined up in darkness. Sam and Lisa took the wrong cart by mistake and hit a concrete curbing on their way home. "Dad, the curb jumped in front of our cart!" Fender bender with a stranger's cart. A problem. But where's our cart?... and it's only, only... Day Two!

The next morning? After a rough negotiation with the cart rental guy, I covered the damages. $500. Found our cart #47. All good, all good. All clear! Back to the beach, Stress Points fading from memory as the splendor of this place washes over us. Amidst it all. Monday (Saturday and Sunday, too) was the best time with my three girls. Ever. The sun opened for a glorious day. Had lunch at "SipSip", the super place on the beach. Dinner at "The Landings." Just great... But after this trip? Second mortgage application in the mail.

Harbor Island is simply magical... unique. All the stress points here are so easy to absorb. Even those above. Three "Daze" on Harbour Island. What would you expect? Here? What do you care?

# CULTURE TRUMPS
# STRATEGY EVERYTIME

*Sometimes we make the mistake of prejudging someone. Kinda.*
*Here's an encounter with a guy where this applied in some ways...*
*not others. You'll see what I mean.*

After 50+ years of building and working with teams, I have learned one indisputable thing. *Culture trumps strategy... every time.*

Early in 2017, I had lunch with a guy a client of mine asked me to interview for him. The guy arrived in a three-piece suit, twenty minutes late... loquacious. He talked for 45 minutes. Home in Carmel, apartment in New York. Maserati. All of it. You get it.

Then this...

"Steve Jobs was my first client. He led me to Jeff Immelt at GE, Bob Iger at Disney, and I'm working with Rupert Murdoch to transition his sons into his empire."... "Check please!" Did I really have to listen to this guy any further? What would I tell my client? Oh well. I actually had experienced worse before, so I sat and listened some more.

He went on. Strategy, tactics, goals, profits, infrastructure, insufferable egos. All the stuff he dealt with while advising his elite list of consulting clients. My instant response, "Zzzzz"... I was done entertaining his falsehoods.

Thankfully, after this soliloquy, my guest ran out of breath. I hadn't acknowledged or responded to any of his claims. He was looking for breathless reactions from me that never came. While catching his breath, he uttered, "And...? (he'd forgotten my name), what do you do?"

My turn... "Well? All those incredibly important things that you address with your clients? I deal with the human dynamics that impact them all. I 'lubricate' the system so all the parts you describe work fluidly. I help people work together more effectively. More aligned. Make teams work better by helping them collaborate, create... perform at top levels. Behaviors, communication. All the "soft stuff" so many organizations fail to dignify. Give a lot of lip service, too, but act upon far less. I refer to this as the "invisible" phase of the business process. That cultural part of a business that is hard to quantify."

"In the work I do, I firmly believe CULTURE TRUMPS STRATEGY... EVERY TIME."

My lunch guest was stunned. I was stunned that he looked stunned! Could this be a revelation to Mr. Big? Was he actually impressed by this brief claim of mine? Maybe it was the way I described it? He relaxed a bit in his chair. "That's fascinating! Can we have lunch next week?" I was having foot surgery. "Sorry, I cannot." I paid the check and said, "Call me next week, and we'll find a date." We parted. I never heard from him again.

I went home right after lunch. Curious. Thought I'd Google this guy. Huh!? Everything he'd told me at lunch was true. Jobs, Murdoch... all of it! I had just had lunch with one of the premier business consultants in America. Based on what he shared during our time together, I would have loved to "shadow" him some time, and witness what he and his work with his elite clientele really looked like.

While I may have been unimpressed with his ego... the way he delivered his message, I had a renewed confidence that the work I was dedicating my life to have value.

Culture first... the strategy follows. CULTURE TRUMPS STRATEGY... EVERY TIME. I wrote this down years ago. Its relevance is more true today than ever:

After working on strategy for 20 years, I can say this. The best strategy means nothing in isolation. If the strategy conflicts with what people believe, it will fail. Conversely, a culturally robust team can turn a so-so strategy into a winner.

Thank you, my friend. Through the pain of listening to you... I learned so much.

# The Fahey Cup

*I've been fortunate to experience so many great things over decades.
Maybe no single experience has been more fun than my twenty-plus years
annually joining my college fraternity brothers
to gather in celebration of "The Fahey Cup."*

The first "Fahey Cup" took place in 2002 at Essex Country Club outside Boston. A group of my fraternity brothers from our alma mater, Trinity College, came up with a novel idea... *"Why don't we invite all our old fraternity brothers to play golf and have dinner sometime?"* One of them was an Episcopal priest. Fitting... as I think the Lord had a hand in birthing what has become a very special, unique experience.

Twenty or so of us gather every year at some of the premier golf destinations in the country. We play golf, mostly bad... no one cares. Began as a revisit of our days at our fraternity, Alpha Delta Phi. Renewing old friendships, trading old jokes and jabs we enjoyed while there. You get it... "Fahey" was named for our infamous, irreverent frat cook, Edward Fahey. One of the grossest guys on earth. "How 'bout a twatta, Bobby."... "The Lincoln Tunnel with a fur collar." (Both inside really gross jokes). Ed was a real character. Just one of the truly lascivious guys who ever walked the earth. Who could have imagined how the fun of "The Fahey" would evolve over the years, honoring a guy like Ed. Such were our college days.

You see, we showed up in 2002 and took up right where we left off at graduation. All the jabs and jokes, of course. But we would also share what had happened over the 40yrs we'd been apart. Fascinating. What amazed me most was how little self-promotion, "look at me", big ego stuff took place. Turned out we were all "successful" in so many different and interesting ways. "Fahey" was rich with the counsel to Major League Baseball... Presidents, CEOs of this company and that... the 25-year coach of soccer and tennis at Yale University. Wall Street guys. Three Episcopal priests! On and on. Accomplished all, but with it a lot of humility, too.

We've had guest speakers. Tucker Carlson from Fox News. The legendary squash coach at our college, Paul Assaiante. And one of our very own, "The Birdman" Whose hilarious remembrances of our years at Trinity have been signature. Last year we were at Yale University. Steve Griggs, the retired soccer coach, organized this one for us. Highlighted by a magical concert delivered by the Whiffenpoofs. Yale's legendary men's singing group. Incredible. Each "Fahey" brother who has hosted us has brought us something new. Always something special to each event.

We're known to one another by our nicknames. Get this. Chief, Sleepy, Moon, Puss, Satch, Poor, Griggsy, Skipper, Derm, Cheels, Straps, Houner, Stroke, Wighty, Jake, Tomato, Foxy, Chaps, Birdman, G&G, Wrecker, chrome, Schweitz, Grundy, Dawser. What has emerged from sixteen consecutive "Faheys?" Most importantly, deep friendships. An intimacy among us that men rarely experience... becomes more meaningful as we move on.

Several dear brothers have left us... passed away. In truth, we are all on the "back nine." George Andrews, our leader, told me at our first Fahey, "Bricks, someday Fahey may be a foursome." A bit sad to think about maybe, but great motivation, too, for all of us to just be there... each and every year. For each "Fahey."

Don't know where we'll be this year, but I always love seeing my great friends. The "Fahey" lives on. Brothers, all on the "back nine"... locking arms with jabs, jokes, and smiles. Hugs. Some tears along the way, too. Let's celebrate what our one-of-a-kind "Fahey Cup" truly is. A gathering of guys. Unique for sure. But an expression of caring for one another that will last for our lifetimes.

# Did Ya Ever See a Dead Man Fall Out of a Window?

*This is an absolute riot!*

My grandfather was a genuine character. Every Sunday "Pop" would drive from his apartment in Germantown, Philadelphia to our home in the 'burbs. He'd come to have dinner with us. One time as he arrived he had to "relieve himself"... after all, he was in his 70s. Pop was slight. About 5' 6"... Stooped over by arthritis. Three-piece suit always. Horn-rimmed glasses, always a cigar dangling from his mouth. Get the picture?

He returned from the bathroom after relieving himself. His fly was down. "Hey, Pop... your zipper's down, you're at "half-mast." He glanced over stooped over with a wry smile and that cigar dangling from his mouth, he mumbled, *"What are you worried about? Dya ever see a dead man fall out of a window?"*

Hilarious! Where did the classics like my Pop go? The jokes, the spontaneity, that simple, wonderful joyous way of living life. Always so plain-spoken... just fun. Many I can remember. Jonathan Winters, John Wayne, Harry Truman, Johnny Carson. These few just jump into my mind. Who would you add? You know the truth-tellers. Hilarious until you could laugh no more. Of course, they operated with a lot less interference, "Noise." The pace of life was so much slower! They could live with a routine. Up early, home early. Dinner with family most days?

Oh, the vices were there. Alcohol. We didn't know as much about the dangers then. Smoking. Until the smoking ban in the early '60s, we would live in the smell, the passive smoke almost anywhere. God only knows the sickness it may have caused.

But that's what we knew then. Cars drove slower. Music lyrics of the time we're understandable. Sinatra, Como, Crosby. We had our morning newspapers, a milkman... can you imagine? My father, a classic, was irreverent like my grandfather. Loud. Mention "Love" to him? He'd say, "Phooey! Love is for sissies." He always watched "Paladin," the Friday night fights, and World War II documentaries. Not a touchy-feely guy at all. But he loved us so. Most of the men of that era felt that loving was for women. The mantra? Men should never cry... women should never get angry. So much for that today, huh?

I often harken back to the memories. Remembering my grandfather and my dad. Both classic characters were. The feelings I have for my Pop are still vivid, everlasting, really. By the way. The dead man never did fall out of the window!

We all laughed until we cried!

# Tears

*Never apologize for tears. You never know what may cause tears. The sight of the Atlantic Ocean can do it, or a piece of music, or a face you've never seen before. A pair of somebody's old shoes can do it. Almost any movie - a horse cantering across a meadow, the high school basketball team running out onto the gym floor. You can never be sure. But of this you can be sure. Whenever you find tears in your eyes, especially unexpected tears, it is well to pay close attention.*

*They are telling you something about the secret of who you are. Often God is speaking to you through them about the mystery of from where you have come and is summoning you to where you should go next* if your soul is to be saved,

*There are moments when true authenticity shows up. Such was the case when Bret Baier spent the last hours with one of the great minds of our time...* Charles Krauthammer, who died on June 21, 2018.

America has lost a hero. This term may be overused. But Charles Krauthammer was certainly a hero. He died in 2018. Charles was the essence of integrity, authenticity, and grace. FoxNews aired a special last Friday. A rich, vibrant recounting of Krauthammer's life. Told mostly by him in a reserved, soft-spoken manner. Shared openly based on the facts of his life. More clinical. Less cathartic and emotional. I found my eyes filling the entire hour. But here is the point of this message. Bret Baier, a FoxNews anchor, interviewed Charles during the program. Brett is a solid professional. He delivers news objectively, with little emotion every evening at 6 pm.

Obviously deeply connected to Charles, he closed the interview by reading a message Krauthammer had sent only to him conveying the news that he, Charles, had but a few weeks to live. Baier later shared this with the world and with those who so loved and respected this incredible man.

Baier read the message... his head down. As he came to the last few sentences, you could hear his voice tremble. Brett had worked through his own great personal struggles with a son who was living with severe heart problems.

Then this. He raised his head, tears streaming down his cheeks. So many times, you will see someone pause at this moment and apologize, "Sorry... Can't believe I'm so emotional." Or they wave their hand in front of their face, drying their tears. But Baier never flinched. Never apologized. As his tears streamed, you could feel the depth of his emotions. Vulnerably, his tears flowed... unapologetically. A clear reflection of the depth of his feelings for his great friend. Bret Baier did not apologize for his tears that evening. We should never apologize for ours either.

# Ocean

*In keeping with emotional experiences like the last piece, I offer a reflection
I recently had to capture. A "firefly" moment struck...
stunned really by the magnificence of the ocean.*

Vast... shimmering... always active. But soothingly so. A gorgeous,
sparkling blue. This is the ocean. In all its wonderment. Its essence?... a
fully spiritual phenomenon. An experience for me, like no other. Nancy
and I are in Palm Beach, Florida for a few days celebrating the birthday of
a dear friend. You cannot go to PB without visiting the Breakers. Henry

Flagler's 1896 gem, nestled on the Atlantic. An imposing hotel and floral feast that despite its grandeur... is still upstaged by the ocean it sits on. The ocean has been a signature part of my life. A source of calm. A constant assurance for me that God exists. Just think about this: Over 70% of our world is ocean, water. There are 343 million trillion (quintillion) gallons of water that cover our earth. To imagine any being, human or otherwise that could create the oceans? Well, you try. I cannot.

Every time I set my toes in the sand and walk to the water, I feel like I'm reuniting with an old friend. Awestruck. Find it hard to comprehend. The waves. Oh, the constancy of the waves. Rolling in and rolling out. In and out. Forever. They talk to me. It's a conversation really. Few things in life have no measure. Are just fathomless. The firmament. The stars and galaxies for sure. The ocean. It comes to us softly, violently even. Its rhythmic, melodic sound is always there. Familiar to me. Always opens me so. The message that comes to me when I'm with the ocean? Simply, "God is." Whenever I go to the ocean, I'm always compelled to be with the ocean.

I'll go there this afternoon. Take a few deep breaths. Even dive in and ride a few waves. The saltwater always revives and rejuvenates me. Even the taste of the salty water enhances my swim.

God gives us oceans. Who knows what their mysteries might provide us someday? I'll just continue to go to the water. As so many millions do every year. But for every one of us, our visits will help us grow... if only a tiny bit each time. For me? Each time I'm with the ocean, I'm moved. Sent on my path with a little more energy. Fueled by the confidence that God is real. He is with me. And like the ocean... always.

# AS THE ROAD NARROWS

*I value just "being" today... far more than "doing." I think it's because "being" allows me to remember and savor all the "doing" I've done over seventy-five years. By just "being."*

No intention to be maudlin here. Just the opposite.

I just celebrated my 75th birthday. As I move along "the back nine" of my life, a lot of changes. I'm more emotional. More nostalgic. More thoughtful... reflective. The gap between what I've wanted and what I have is closing. I think I know more now. Know better who I really am.

Some other things too...

Eye contact with others is different... softer, engaged longer. Eyes often moist. Always joined with a smile. "Cocktail" talk has been replaced by more "real" conversation. A common, unspoken feeling knowing that my peers and I are traveling the same narrowing road. All with a "let's make things count" attitude. Then there are those grandchildren. Oh my, those grandchildren. You appreciate that all life experiences are gifts. When more of life is in your rear-view mirror than on your windshield, feelings intensify. Rather than run through life like a drunken sailor, I need to see time as finite. Moments are to be savored. Pausing along the way... is a gift unto itself.

As the saying goes... "As the body declines... the spirit grows." Good. But this is like anything else. You have to be aware this will be so. Working to build spiritual strength is a choice, optional. Losing physical strength is not. I hear people lament, "It's hard getting old." Or "What would you expect from someone my age?" Or "Getting old isn't easy." Age is not just a number. It's a reality. But it's up to you to choose your own perspective on all this. Think positively or negatively. Are your days nourishing or draining? Your choice.

My best years have been my later years. Probably post 60. Why? I think it's because I approach each new day now as more of a gift than a... "there's always tomorrow" thing. I have some health issues. None of which are life-threatening. At least not now. Some aches and pains. Okay. Part of the deal as I move on.

My career has careened back and forth over fifty-plus years. Maybe a three steps forward, two steps back thing. But always more learnings from my losses than my gains. Wisdom emerges amidst all the successes and setbacks. I feel the urge to share what I've learned with others. Distribute it to my coachies... my grandkids, for sure. I find this creates a more enchanting life for me.

Friendships... friendships... friendships. The best of these become part of me. Are irreplaceable companions as the road narrows. Some of my best friends are gone. Some have lost spouses or children. Some are ill. Some severely. I lost a brother who drown at age two. A roommate from college who died at age 28. Four dear fraternity brothers who died in their 60s. You can track through your own losses, I'm sure.

These losses only make my appreciation of my life more vibrant. Yeah, a little "could be me" passes by each time I hear of a friend facing a setback, experiencing a tragedy. But I believe it's always best to keep moving. "Run through the tape." Finish the race well. My motto? "Stay the Course!" It's my constant urging to those I coach. Staying in motion physically, mentally, and spiritually is crucial.

Years ago, there was a TV show focused on aging... featuring a group of people over the age of 70. "Over Easy" explored how we see things... as the road narrows. One question posed during one show?

"If you could change two things in your life as you look back on the years, what would they be?" What were the two answers offered most?

1. I wish I'd taken more risks.

2. I wouldn't have taken myself so seriously.

How would you answer the questions posed here?

Lastly, a friend of mine... simply passing by one day, asked this with a wry smile, "Bob, you know how a shark dies? It stops swimming." So as my road narrows, I celebrate all the blessings. Know God's grace may be with me someday.

My hope is you can process all you have experienced as well. As your road narrows, what a beautiful way to "hit the tape."

# BⲈN FRANKLIN

*The quote below should remind us all that we have a choice at key moments in time. To see either a rising or setting sun. Our perspective, our attitude facing what we're dealing with will be largely determinant of the ultimate outcome. This could not be truer today...*

Whilst the last members were signing the Constitution.

Doctor Franklin, while looking towards the President's Chair, at the back of which had been painted a rising sun? He observed that painters had found it difficult to distinguish in their art a *rising from a setting* sun.

"I have often, and often in the course of the Session, and the vicissitudes of my hopes and fears as to its issue, looked at that figure behind the President without being able to tell whether it was rising or setting: But now at length, I have the happiness to know that it is a *rising and not a setting sun.*"

# He Never Hit Back

*I deal with a lot of conflict between people in my coaching practice. Anger can fuel it, even rage at times. The "I'll get even with him" theme surfaces all the time. My usual counsel? Take the high road. No need to hit back. This next piece will illustrate what I mean...*

Our President Trump, "He Hits Back!"

Oh, does he ever! But what if he didn't? At least not quite as hard or as often? Let me share a story that may help address this question. Legendary hockey player Mark Messier starred in the National Hockey League for a quarter of a century from 1984 to 2009. During his inspiring career, he was much admired. What is less known? He was also acutely vilified.

Messier owns a wonderful boutique hotel on the magical island of Harbor Island in the Bahamas. Nancy and I go there every year. Mark's sister Jennifer manages the place. One day, Jennifer and I were chatting at the bar. "Tell me a little about you, Jen." The usual acquainting stuff two might go through. She told me a little about herself. Fascinating. Her family, her career. Then Jennifer shared this with me. When her brother Mark played for the New York Rangers in the early '90s, there was a sportswriter who made it his purpose to take Mark Messier down. Report negatively about him. Jennifer indicated this guy published nothing but slurs and lies in the New York press about Mark for years.

The sportswriter's attacks on Messier, according to Jennifer, were unrelenting. On and on. But despite these attacks, Mark never retaliated. Never took his opponent's "bait." He simply continued to serve as captain of his team, leading the Rangers to its first Stanley Cup in 54 years. All this, as his arch-critic continued to write negatively about who Mark Messier was. But Messier? *He never hit back.*

But here's the wonderful irony in all this. The sportswriter eventually retired. Maybe he'd run out of breath going after Mark. As he left his job... after all the years attacking Mark. In his final article, he wrote this, and I take license with my words:

"I've crucified Mark Messier in the press for years. His family, his fidelity to his wife, his team, his reputation. Really terrible stuff. Amazingly, Mark never hit back at me. He never hit back. Mark Messier is one of the finest, most upstanding people I've ever known. Faced with all I said about him over many years. The negative impact I tried to have on him and his career... he never lashed out. He possesses personal character and courage that are rare today. Mark Messier is a very good guy.

You have to defend yourself at times. But hitting back always invites more hitting. Fight hate with hate? Maybe not. Turning the other cheek? Hmm. Mark Messier took the higher road. The guy who tried to vanquish him failed to win. In the final resolve, Messier stood tall... simply amazing.

# ENOUGH

*A new year always calls each of us to new commitments. We set new goals. Most of the time, they're too lofty. Unreachable. But we make them anyway in our pursuit of more... always more. Never fully satisfied. Here's an interesting perspective on "more" and the happiness we hope it will bring. But rarely does. We will always have, and we are always, Enough.*

Coaching has revealed many important truths for me. One most prevalent is the fact that few people do what they say they will do. They

plan, they commit. But most of the time they fall short. Robert Browning, in a famous poem, says, "A man's reach should exceed his grasp." But I wonder. May things outside our grasp prevent us from reaching the very happiness we're looking for. Do we unknowingly set ourselves up for failure by chasing our ideal? Seeking perfection? Have goals that are too lofty, only attainable if we say, hit the lottery? All in the pursuit of more. More wealth, more status... just more and more of a lot of things.

Jack Bogle was the founder of "Vanguard", one of the largest financial services companies in the world. He was an icon in the financial services industry. His character, stature, and presence as a leader? Unparalleled.

But a brief story about Jack I once heard said more about our ideals, goal setting, our constant pursuit of more, hoping to find happiness, than anything I've ever learned.

Jack and a friend were walking on a beach in South Hampton, Long Island one Summer. This is one of the wealthiest spots in the country. Jack's friend turned to him and said, "Hey, Jack, how's it make you feel that the guy in that thirty-million-dollar mansion over there makes more in a day... than you make in a year?"

Bogle looked directly at his friend and replied, "That may be true. But, ya know? I've got something that guy will never have." His friend puzzled by Bogle's response asked curiously, "What's that, Jack?"

"I've got enough, my friend... I've got enough."

What a wonderful lesson. So much is written today about the pursuit of happiness. Usually tied to the material things in life. Always more. We're always looking for more.

We've all heard this before.

"Someday, I'll sit back and be satisfied with all I've earned. All I've accomplished. All I've acquired. Someday I'll enjoy the fruits of my labors."

Jack Bogle died three years ago, a wealthy man, at the age of 89. His only regret about his money? "I'm just sorry I didn't have more to give away." Bogle gave half of his annual Vanguard salary to charity."

# CHAPTER 6
# COACHINGS

# COACHINGS

*I mentioned that I'm in the "distributive" phase of my life. Candidly, my mortality comes to mind as I write this. Why? Because when I look at my "toolbox" of exercises and concepts I've utilized over decades...*
*I realize I have 500 files on my computer! I used to be a pitcher.*
*Modestly, a pretty good one, I think. Batters found it hard to hit me.*
*Usually because batters never knew what to expect. We have hard things, unexpected things we all face. There are tools, concepts... coaching tips that can assist when dealing with problems that may stump you.*
*I offer here just a few of those coaching tools I've created. Mostly borrowed.*
*That I've employed over decades. Try some of them. They work.*

# Quiet Time

*There are so many instructional coaching tips out there. "Do this; do that." These are good. Important. But contrary to actions you can take is this... "Quiet Time."*

    I began CONNECTIONS describing my mornings. The "fireflies" that almost imperceptibly come by as I quiet myself early in my day and just "Be." Versus "Do." Silence. Only God knows what we will be, where we will be when we leave this earth. But can we sense and receive "whispering" messages if we silence ourselves and are open? As those "fireflies" may flicker by? I have found this to be profoundly true.

But I've also found this "quieting" myself isn't easy. I've learned over years that "being" is critical preparation for the "doing" that will follow. Tasks that will occupy the day that follows.

So, what might you do to quiet yourself? Be open to receive, quietly...

1.  Get up early. When the rest of the family sleeps. You just need to be alone with you.

2.  Soft music? Coffee? Your favorite place to sit.

3.  Still Yourself; close your eyes or focus your eyes on something; breathe slowly (meditation? Kinda.)

4.  Shhhh... wait. "Where did that come from?"... "Another."

5.  No messages?   It may take a number or maybe many times before you receive anything. Okay. The simple pause, quieting yourself is beneficial whether "fireflies" come your way right away or not.

6.  This is not an exercise. A project seeking a specific result. Rather it is an invitation to just be with yourself. For three, five, ten minutes. Time is really no issue. I suggest you begin... maybe two, three times a week. Then silence yourself as the spirit moves.

What follows are exercises. Things you can do. Just remember. The more you ready yourself of what is to be done... quietly. The more effective those "dos" will be.

# Uncovering

*I think it's important to know that we rarely discover who we are. We "uncover" who we are. It takes a lifetime of work to evolve. The process starts inside and works its way out. God creates a sacred center in all of us. He then gives us the choices that lead us to grow... develop and become who we are intended to become.*

We've all dreamed "what if... "

"What if I left this job?" Or. "If only I'd invested in___? "What if?"
So many possibilities. Just dreams? Well, maybe they don't have to be.

Have you ever sat quietly by yourself wondering? "What if?" If you
deepen your thoughts, you may hear faint little "whispers." I call them
"fireflies." Calling you to heed thoughts about your future. These
"what ifs" may be more within your reach than you think.

"Can you help me find, discover what's next?" A perfectly honest
question that I get a lot. People I coach who commit to their personal
growth are always seeking their "next level."

They feel the urge to keep moving forward. "I've got an itch, an
inkling this isn't my last step." It's out there.

Let's look. Out there. What's next for him among the myriad of
possibilities? Whether it be a career change or a transformation to a
vastly new life. As I was told decades ago... if you're willing to dream
and most importantly, take a risk? "The world can be your oyster."

So, on to a real-life example.

This guy has a lot on his plate. A career with a major international
company. Beautiful family; strong sense of self. He's a horse. I love his
spirit. How intentional he is about living. What can I do for him? Help
him acknowledge the subtleties "whispering" to him amidst the flurry
of his full, well-lived life.

Now he's a planner. Thinks methodically about his future. Unusual.
But this provides an exceptional opportunity for him to surface his
"what ifs." He tells me he has thoughts every once in a while. Even
dreams about being out of the large company rat race, running his own
boutique consulting firm. "But this is really unrealistic," he tells me. I
tell him, let's take a closer look at that. Think back. How many times
have you entertained these thoughts? Are they becoming more vivid?
Have you truly assessed the possibility of living your dream?"

In fact, my friend has been drawn to these thoughts for years.
Complicated by the awkward politics and bureaucracy impeding his
current role as an advisor. It's like a floating puzzle in his head.
He's never taken the time to bring the pieces together. I tell him,
"Hypothetically, let's pull these images down and put them on paper."

He does, and we pull the pieces together. Build a timeline and a financial plan. How he might make connections that can lead him to materialize this more clearly.

I was watching Novak Djokovic accept this year's Wimbledon trophy.

"As a very young boy, my father put a tennis racket in my hands. Immediately I saw green grass. Little did I know that experience led me to this place. I was that young boy who dreamed of playing Wimbledon one day."

Both my friend and Novak Djokovic had "uncovered" what was already inside them. A gift we can all aspire to receive. If we have the desire, the wisdom to capture the spirit

At some point in life, you want to identify your passion. When you do, life changes. However distant or difficult it may be to do so. You don't want to look back someday and regretfully say to yourself... "If only."

# 14 DON'TS OF HIGHLY SUCCESSFUL PEOPLE

*This is a "takeoff" on Stephen Covey's "Seven Habits of Highly Effective People." Only here are "14 Don'ts of Highly Successful People."*

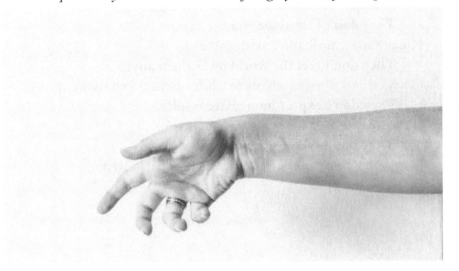

**14 Don'ts of Highly Successful People**
- **They don't waste time feeling sorry for themselves.**
(You're never a victim.)
- **They don't shy away from change.**
(Change is a choice. Not a matter of capacity.)

· **They don't give away their power.**
(You must always hold your "space.")
· **They don't focus on things they can't control.**
(You cannot change one molecule in another person.)
· **They don't worry about pleasing everyone.**
(Pleasers unfortunately avoid conflict resolution.)
· **They don't fear taking calculated risks.**
(Emotional risks above all.)
· **They don't dwell on the past.**
(It's about the windshield, not the rear-view mirror.)
· **They don't make the same mistakes over and over.**
(They know you only win and learn, not win, or lose.)
· **They don't resent other people's success.**
(It's always about you... your success only.)
· **They don't give up after the first failure.**
(If you fire at the target and miss, you fire again.)
· **They don't fear alone time.**
(Quiet time... meditation. Both are key.)
· **They don't feel the world owes them anything.**
(They take total responsibility for their successes and failures.)
· **They don't expect immediate results.**
(Patience is a rare commodity these days.)
· **They don't fail to execute.**
(They are accountable. The results are the final judge.)

# High Trust/Low Maintenance

*Important we pause occasionally and assess where we stand with another. How are we doing? Is the relationship healthy or is it strained? What might I want to do to build trust with another? So, there will be less emotional maintenance I need to apply to make it more fluid? Healthy...*

**High Trust/Low Maintenance**

Leadership is art more than science. One thing I've noticed about the best leaders I've worked with. They can build trust in those they connect with. Quickly. Whether it's tone, eye contact, or whatever. People gravitate to them. Quickly.

This allows outstanding leaders to spread their influence to others. Establish a "connectedness" that can be infectious. These high trust (HT) relationships bring with them a low maintenance (LM) quality as well. There is less need to continue to prove oneself to a colleague or fellow employee. Trust is solidly in place. No drawn-out... over-engaged interaction to bring people alongside is required. Leaders able to create HT/LM relationships quickly are better, more influential, and more successful.

Is there a trick or knack to this? Well, no. We often ask, "Are leaders born or made?" I think the answer is both. The ability to connect with others comes from an innate sense of caring... resulting usually in a healthy, trust-based relationship. You cannot fake sincerity, authenticity. In a real sense, people "feel" these qualities in another. They trust quickly. Question and doubt less. Makes a relationship flow more smoothly.

HT/LM... you might think about the relationships you enjoy. Are they high trust/low maintenance or conversely are they low in trust/high in, requiring a lot of maintenance?

# CONFLICT MANAGEMENT EXERCISE

*I have spent most of my years working with people helping resolve differences between them. Business families, or just between those unable to disentangle from the differences they are dealing with. The conflict management exercise below (CSS) provides a structure to prevent finger-pointing, blame. Instead helps objectify the issues and allows each party to accept their responsibility for the conflict.*

### Conflict Management Exercise

**Continue...**                    **Stop...**                    **Start...**

Conflict between individuals can be one of the most distracting, disabling problems a business can face. It can surface between fellow employees as well as between an employee and his or her employer. In either case, early resolution is important in order to restore productivity for both the individuals and the business itself.

Conflict, when managed properly, is not negative. In its simplest form, conflict is nothing more than the difference between what one has and what one wants.

Note that conflict does not mean hostility. Hostility is actually a conflict avoidance technique practiced by individuals who really don't want to resolve issues that have created the conflict.

One technique that has proven to be successful in assisting people deal with conflict is an exercise known as CONTINUE/STOP/START.

Conducted one on one, the CSS exercise gets to core issues that might not be addressed otherwise through normal discourse.

### The Steps of the CSS Exercise are:

1. Each person takes time to assess the issues impacting the relationship they have with an individual with whom they are in conflict. Each then records on a sheet of paper three or four things they would like the other person to "continue" doing, three or four things they would like the person to "stop" doing, and three or four things they would like the other person to "start" doing. Focus should be on behaviors.

2. In a face-to-face session, each individual reads or tells the other what they have observed or concluded. The receiving party cannot respond until the sender completes his or her observations. When he or she responds, it should only be to clarify, not disagree or defend.

3. The process is then reversed, and the sender becomes the receiver and vice versa.

4. They make an action plan and set a review date. This will typically be three to four months hence but maybe sooner if the need is more urgent to do so.

5. The real value comes through a series of CSS exercises as trust and openness grow.

### The CONTINUE / STOP / START Exercise

Reflecting on the relationship you have with _____ clearly and specifically record below your observations as instructed above.

**CONTINUE:**

1.

2.

3.

**STOP:**

1.

2.

3.

**START:**

1.

2.

3.

Based on the exercise completed and what I have learned about myself I commit to the following actions to improve the relationship I have with _____. What actions should be taken?

# MARGIN

*One stroke... one last-second 3-pointer. That overtime field goal. A competition can last four hours or four days. More times than not, it inevitably comes down to a thin-margin ending. Margin. Personal growth exists on the margin, too. Look at this...*

*A behavioral edge can be the difference between win and loss. Competency and inadequacy...*

Here is one of the most impactful teachings I pass on to all my coachies.

Those who come to me for help have a lotta guts. It's not easy to open yourself up to someone you don't know well. But vulnerability and trust are kissin' cousins. Share and learn. Converse with another and you will grow. If trust can build early between a coachie and me, we're usually "off to the races."

But with them all, there's always a sense of doubt and hurt. A feeling of in some way being "lesser than." They ask, "Why can't I be happier? Like myself more?" There are varying degrees of this. But these thoughts are usually resident.

So, what about "Margin?"

Many years ago I went to my dermatologist for some skin cancer removal. "Mr. Brickley, if the margins are clear, we know the cancer is gone." Made me think.

*If the margins are clear*, It might be a great coaching lesson.

We are all God's children. He has imbued in each of us the need, desire to live our lives. A life our heart desires. At our core, 85% of you/me is solid. Good. Able to fully take on life's challenges. As a coach, I don't help them remake themselves. It's never about an overhaul. It's about refinement, just tuning the "engine." It's all about the "margin."

I'll spend four or five hours early on getting to know a coachie. From family background to career... from key relationships to values. All of it. In truth, in 100% of the cases, I conclude and share this. "I have some great news for you. You're going to be an easy one for me. 85% of you is okay. Just fine." I love the sense of relief. Added confidence in their faces when I tell them this.

I continue ...

Coaching you is a lot like music. You can buy very good music today for a few hundred dollars. $300? $500 perhaps. And you get... maybe 85% of it. But if you want that last 15%? It'll cost you $5000. That marginal, extra difference is special. Something only a trained ear will savor. The margin here... makes a huge difference."

Margins in us amplify who we really are. To make my point. Think of a flickering flame. If you fan it, a full fire follows. If you make small changes, marginal changes in you... like fire... they will spread through all of you.

Lastly, I think of sports. I'm reminded of the year Matt Ryan, the Falcons' star quarterback, underperformed. Everything about him looked fine. What happened? During the off-season, he discovered his footwork when passing was just slightly off. After a small marginal adjustment? Good result. A little more confidence? Matt followed with his best year ever.

Behaviors... discipline... clarity of purpose... values. So many issues that make up the person in front of me. It's about refining these. Taking the time to find that little extra. That added 15%. The margin makes all the difference.

And when we do? It's like watering a beautiful plant and watching it flourish. By addressing the margins. Growth follows... and then I just love seeing people blossom.

# FAMILIARS

*So many of us get stuck in a pattern of behavior. A Kind of "Groundhog Day" syndrome. But when in this loop, it is usually hard for one to see it. Know how harmful cycling through the same behavior pattern over and over… can really be. While breaking a recycling behavior pattern can be difficult, doing so will spawn new growth… forward progress.*

From time to time, I find myself in places when I feel "stuck" … you know, lacking motivation, energy. You too? Routines repeat, over and over most days. Behaving in ways that may be helpful. But also, those that are not. Why? Because they are familiar to me. Maybe that's it. They are just familiar. Form a pattern that's hard to alter, break.

Don't get me wrong. Repetitive routines are helpful and healthful. Most times. Getting up to start a day… exercising… following a healthy diet. But there are also other routines that can take me down.

The *familiar* is a <u>feeling</u> that we unconsciously reproduce over and over again. This feeling causes us to do things that are not productive or smart… may be even self-destructive. But our impulse to reproduce the *familiar* is so strong that we do so regardless of the negative behaviors that result.

The key here is to identify your current *familiars* and work to replace them with healthier, more productive *familiars* moving forward.

1.  Write down two recurring feelings you experience that cause you to act or make decisions that may not be healthy.

2.   What made you choose the familiar feelings you did?


3.   Can you trace their origin and see the specific times you have reproduced these *familiars*? If so, explain the origin and the circumstances.


4.   If you could replace your current *familiars* with more positive, healthful feelings, what would they be? Describe them in detail.


Identifying behaviors that may result in inefficiency, unnecessary emotional strife? Eliminating these can remove obstacles to growth. Try this.

# VΛLUҽS ҽXҽRCISҽ

I've lived the past twenty-five years guided by three core principles:
*People...*

I've been dedicated to working with people. I'm fascinated by the human dynamics that make different people "tick." Many times, when working with a business client, they would ask me to design a succession process for a next phase of ownership, leadership or help rebuild their business infrastructure. Mechanics? Structural stuff. But the structural stuff; the mechanics? Not me. "Sorry, my focus is on your people. Who they are. The value they contribute to the business. How the team works together. The quality of the leadership. That's my sweet spot. That's my focus." People.

*Impact...*

Why would I coach someone or a team and have no impact? I wouldn't. I don't. Early on with a new coachie, I would always present them with a simple contract for how we would work together.

1.   If at any time during our time together, you feel I'm not deleting the value you expected, you can stop. In the middle of a sentence if you choose to. But know too, if I determine our work together is not having the impact I expect, I can quit too. This allows us both to have something at risk as our work progresses.

2.   I have a "10 Minute Rule." If you are ten minutes late to a meeting, we cancel.

That's it. No documentation. No fee structure in writing. I'm a great believer in building a relationship with a client based on trust. This approach has served me well for over twenty-five years. Impact.

*Truth...*

After decades of engagement in your special area of "expertise", there's a tendency to think you have all the answers. Your answers. But when coaching, it's critical you get to your client's truth. Not to impose your own on him/her. We always value a professional more for the questions he or she asks than the answers provided. I always say, "You learn nothing while you're talking." Truth... get to the client's truth as fully as possible. The process is never about you... always about them.

At work, with family or friends. In every circumstance we find ourselves? We make decisions regarding our responses, our behaviors... the choices we make. There is either an instinctive or a declared set of guidelines that show us a desired path. Interestingly, I've found the guidelines need not be fully descriptive or too complex. In fact, to be most effective, think of "threes." Three little pigs. Three blind mice. The Holy Trinity. Threes just work. Thus, I've found is the case with a personal values system. The exercise below helps you uncover your personal values. You don't discover these. You only uncover what's already there. Only three works. A great family exercise to go through. With your business team. Even a one-on-one relationship.

## Uncovering Your Values

*"The most important thing in life is to decide what is most important."*

Who are you? What do you stand for? What are the values by which you operate and treat another? Look over the list of values below. Circle those that "jump out" because of their importance to you. Then write your top three values in the spaces below. Feel free to add your own values if they aren't listed below.

| | | | |
|---|---|---|---|
| Truth | Persistence | Action | Resources |
| Efficiency | Sincerity | Dependability | Initiative |
| Fun | Environmentalism | Trust | Relationships |
| Excellence | Fulfillment | Wisdom | Teamwork |
| Dreams | Flexibility | Service | Courage |
| Perspective | Profitability | Excitement | Competition |
| Commitment | Freedom | Impact | Recognition |
| Friendship | Creativity | Learning | Influence |
| Happiness | Honesty | Justice | Quality |
| Honor | Originality | Innovation | Candor |
| Hard Work | Obedience | Responsiveness | Prosperity |
| Abundance | Financial Growth | Respect | Fulfillment |
| Fairness | Community | Purposefulness | Integrity |
| Advise | Support | Peace | Spirituality |
| Self-Control | Strength | Empathy | Cleverness |
| Clarity | Loyalty | Success | Security |
| Humor | Cooperation | Love | Collaboration |
| Support | Stewardship | | |

**1.**          **2.**          **3.**

# How to Be Memorable

*This is Gracie. My darling golden doodle. From the first time I saw her,
she's never forgotten me. I never forget her. But people are different.
We tend to forget one another. But we all like to be remembered.
So how can we make ourselves more memorable?*

I just love it when someone comes up to me and says, "I remember you!" But I don't remember them.

Thought I'd share a few of my thoughts here. Many of you will relate to these. I'm sure you've used them yourself.

1. I try always to address anyone I encounter by name. Anyone. If I don't know or forget, I'll ask someone. "What's her name?" And then call her by her name. "How'd he know my name?" Always a great start.

2. Always make eye contact. Even when just passing by. Whether it be someone you know. Or yes... even the homeless person on at the highway exit looking for a few bucks.

3. Make 'em all laugh! A quick comment? I usually use sarcasm. Make 'em laugh when few do, or when they're having a tough day? Just give 'em a little chuckle.

4. Write handwritten notes. I try to write two a week. So simple, but today still rarely done. As you "sprinkle" these out, you'll be amazed at how people will remember them.

5. Overtip. Especially those of service who truly enhance an experience. My $20? Usually feels like $50 or more to them.

6. Always keep your head up. Open that radar screen of yours. Scan around. Expect to see someone you know. You usually will.

7. Smile. Smile. And smile some more. People will pick up on your energy. They'll, almost always, smile back. This also gives you a spurt of positivity too.

8. Even if I'm not sure... if someone is even faintly familiar? "Don't I know you?" If so, great! If not, "Oh sorry. I thought you were someone else." No harm done.

9. Be open to the fact that you will run into many you can recognize or reach out to. "Wow, how did you recognize me?! Thanks for reaching out."

10. Lastly, try to always be more interested in them than trying to be interesting yourself.

Be prepared. If you build an inventory of connections with others that are slightly different from the norm? You can expect a lot of, "I remember yous."

Just a few ways to make yourself memorable...

# BETTER... DIFFERENT

*Comparison. Truly one of the relational "traps" we can fall into. Race, ideology... or just other people who don't quite fit into our sphere. Grounded primarily in our human tendency to judge. A solid lesson I learned here...*

I heard long ago... In marketing, you have to be "better or different. Hopefully both." Different from the rest. Better than the rest. That's how you beat the competition, gain market share. A good axiom that has served businesses well. But marketing, winning in business has little to do with my message here.

Rather I want to share with you a caution I've lived with for decades. Personal growth is, just that... personal. We all grow in different ways, at different speeds. Growth fuels feelings of well-being, develops healthy behavior, breeds confidence. Essentially, growth drives much of our success in life.

But here's the caution. Some of us are resistant when it comes to their personal growth. "Oh, that's not for me. Go ahead. You read all those books, take that course. Work with your coach. Not my deal." You can visualize those you know who are like this. Think this way. That's okay. Then there are those who really try to move forward ... healthily. Mentally, physically, spiritually. But their progress seems slow. Slower than yours. Because so much of our lives is built on comparison? Your position in life. It's hard not to compare. Take stock of your status at times. That's okay, too.

"How am I doing relative to him or her?" Joined with this, "Look at me. I'm doing much more than those around me. I'm growing like a weed. Maybe they should just lie down and go to sleep. Look at me go!"

Oops! There it is. The caution. I'm better than all those around me. This is the "negative ego" my coach warns me about frequently. This assertion... "*I'm better!*" will retard growth. Hold you back. Subtle but harmful. *I'm better than all those others."*

I've worked with my coach for decades. I've grown with his guidance. I'm a pretty confident guy.

There are some I know who I love, respect, and can even be in awe of at times, I'll occasionally notice something about them, regardless of their status that surprises me. "I can't believe they didn't know that." Or "Huh, I know that." I'd meet with my coach. "Can you believe they didn't know that?! And that I do?"

Feeling very important as I'm buffing my nails with pride, Coach drills me with this...

*Bob, please know this...*

*"You're going to see those around you who aren't doing the work on their growth like you're doing. It's Ok. In your mind, they may be growing more slowly than you. Know less than you. It's Ok. Or you may look at them and*

*think, "How can they go through life and see themselves not growing at all? Not knowing as much as I do."*

And here's when coach "stones" me! Remember... above all.

*"You are never better than another... only different."*

Wow, what a wake-up call. What a critical aspect of personal growth I needed to embrace... *humility.* Getting too enamored with your status in life... too impressed with who you think you are? What you know. Not good. God made all of us in His image. No one of us is "better" than another. Only "different."

With this lesson, I find myself more accepting, less self-important. More empathetic. Occasionally, I'll admonish myself with this, "Who the hell do you think you are, Bob?! Get over yourself. You don't have all the answers."

No... *"You are never better than another... only different."*

# 85%

*90% of the time this "85%" exercise works. Try it.*

"You know, I just don't know how I can do this anymore." Thus began a challenging conversation I had with a coachie recently. He told me the story about an argument he'd had with his wife. It was over her inability to make decisions. Put things off until the last minute. "She's just driving me nuts!"

It's human nature. No one really likes conflict. Especially with a partner. In business. Personally. Like here with your spouse. We usually know what we want. We may not always know what we need. So we just live with the conflict. My coachie had to decide what he was going to do about the issues, his conflict with his wife.

We began our discussion. "Let's 'T Chart' your relationship with Joan." (Not her real name) That's not him pictured above either!

Take a sheet of paper and draw a vertical line down the middle, top to bottom.

On the right side ... make a list:
- All the negatives ... the gaps in your relationship.
- Things that "bug" you.
- Things you wish she would change.

On the left side ... make a list:
. Why you married ... the day you met her.
- All the things you know about her.
- All she does for you.
- Why you are with her today.
- What you love about her, share together.

He sat there and took ... oh, about five minutes. In 90% of the cases, when one conducts this exercise, the right size dominates. His shoulders dropped. A smile came to his face. "Thanks."

(The 10%? that don't see more on the right than the left? More work to do)

*90% of all those who conducted this exercise. ... 85% or of what they write down is on the left side of the page. Perspective? The lens through which we see things is so determinant of the quality of our daily lives. "Grow weeds or flowers. The choice is yours."*

I offer, "When you look at this, weigh the pluses and the minuses. Can you live with 85%?" In the face of many of the same frustrations with my wife? I've conducted this same exercise. 85%? I'll take it ... any day.

Try it ...

# AWDs

*The little guy here looks a little quizzical, doesn't he?*
*That's because much of what we intend to do... gets done. You know,*
*all those "shoulda, coulda, wouldas." This shows up in my coaching a lot.*
*Where's the accountability? Where's the progress?*
*How do we avoid delay? Our failing to execute.*
*I introduce an accountability process labeled... "AWDs."*

Let me explain.

Much of my interaction with clients centers on meetings with their teams. We cover a lot of ground. As a meeting moves to close, I point out, "We have 5 or 10 minutes left. A number of you are rustling in your seats ready to run out the door to your next thing."

"My question to you is, What was the result of this session?"

Blank stares for the most part.

"Ok, let's take the last few minutes left."

*"What did we learn? And what are we going to do about it?"*

A conversation ensues. Finally, "Good, we've surfaced some valuable learnings. Now, what are we going to do about them?"

On the whiteboard, I write down... AWDs

| **Action** | **Who** | **Deadline** |
| --- | --- | --- |

- Action: What specifically is the task or project identified?

- Who: Who is the one person accountable for completing the action?

  - Only one. He or she may work with others to complete the Action. But only the one person named here is directly accountable for getting it done.

- Deadline: This is the clincher. When will the Action be completed? Not "soon"... "next week"... "when I can." No. What day? Sometimes, what hour of the day? But here's the key. *The only one who sets the deadline is the person above "who" is accountable for completion.* If the boss or someone else sets the deadline? You might hear, "You didn't give me enough time." Sorry, I couldn't meet your deadline." Be sure the person accountable sets their own deadline.

*(Without question... setting deadlines for the work to be done is the most challenging part of this process. Locks in accountability.)*

Follow-Up:  Process always requires a number of meetings to complete Actions. At the beginning of the next meeting? The first agenda item? How did we do completing the tasks identified at our last session? Or do we need to revise the deadlines set previously?

*In other words, no one gets "off the hook."*

"AWDs" ensures things don't fall through the cracks. Locks effective productivity in place.

# About CONNECTIONS

Time to pull this all together.

From... *Preparation, to... Spirituality, to... Relationships, to... People, to... Experiences and More. And finally, to... Coachings.* I've tried to illustrate how my writings are invisibly, magically connected to one another. All have enriched my life with learnings... and I modestly say, some wisdom I hope I've been able to share with you here.

Regardless of which section or piece you may have chosen to read, know above all that CONNECTIONS is dedicated to our reaching out to one another through personal relationships, curiosity, and an openness relate to others, we expand and grow. Every connection with another I've enjoyed, however brief or long-lasting, has enriched my life. In so many unexpected ways. In exciting ways!

As I suggested in my introduction, the best way to read this book is to pick a piece here and there. Many of these are very personal. Others are instructional. Still, others are invitations for you to explore aspects of yourself that you've not considered before. Find "you" at deeper levels of yourself. I hope you have approached this book with this in mind.

Since beginning writing CONNECTIONS, I've become more aware, more mindful of the energy around me. "This happened." "Oh, look at that." ... "Of course, that just happened." "He just gets me." On and on. Very confirming of the connections between us that direct so much of our lives. Continues to build my confidence I've been on the right track.

During my coaching sessions, I'll notice the person in front of me is facing an issue I either read about earlier that day or covered similarly with another coachie in a prior session. These "coincidences" are daily assurances to me that the theme of this book has important relevance. I'll usually take a deep breath and move on. But I'm always taken aback when I end up discussing an issue with someone. And realize I just had the same discussion with another just recently. Common connections are so prevalent... and so real.

I read yesterday that a wonderful teacher at the University of Pennsylvania's Wharton School died of a brain tumor at age 56. Sigal Barsade, a professor of management, urged bosses to think more deeply about emotions, including love, swirling around the workplace.

She cautioned against trying to suppress or ignore emotions at work. "We literally catch emotions from one another like viruses," she said. Viruses. Energy that permeates everything. I've alluded to this in a myriad of ways. Sigal Barsade is just one more example. Indeed, our hopes... our fears... our dreams are always flowing through us. At home, at work. In fact, always. So connected all the time.

So, where do we go from here?

The appeal of CONNECTIONS will vary with each of you who has read any parts of this book. I mentioned earlier. Most of us will pick up a book. Read the first few pages or a piece or two and put it aside. Someone will ask, "Did you read... ?" "Yes, it was great." (Not remembering doing so) But wanting to show how well-read you are? Me? Guilty as charged.

Thus, the structure I chose for CONNECTIONS. Ninety or so bits of chocolate. A "sampler" inviting you to try this one or that one. "Forest Gump-like"... never knowing what you're going to get. I remember the messages in all the stories here. Well, I should. I wrote them all. But I'm asking you to look for those simple takeaways you have had while reading. Maybe... helping you avoid... Things you intend to do, but don't do? Goals you set without deadlines. Personal growth opportunities you never take on. Just stuff that often disappears... just "goes out into the ether." Fades from memory.

If you believe a lot of this is original to me... believe me. It is not. Go read the writings of Marcus Aurelius, a great philosopher, roman emperor from 160-181 AD. Or more recently read John Garner's foundational book <u>Self-Renewal</u>. Stephen Covey's book <u>The Seven Habits of Highly</u>

Successful. People who have reached out to anyone seeking a guidebook for their life. Books that offer much of what I share here.

Writing CONNECTIONS has in large part been self-serving. Writing my blog for the past six years has been truly cathartic. My passion as I've indicated has evolved to be an attempt to impact others ... *help people grow so they will go forth and help others grow.*

As the road narrows traveling my life's path, I have learned one central thing. I've come to the realization of why I wrote CONNECTIONS. Yes, we are all connected. How many you reach out to, strike a relationship with is your personal choice. But doing so is one of the true joys we can experience when we do. I shared with you in an earlier post my picture of my legacy and the scene I visualize as I create it. "The Gathering" pictures all of you. All those I've chosen to connect with right before my eyes. As I leave this earth, I further visualize invisible threads of "energy" attached to each. And by God's grace if that is his desire, I am taken into his loving arms... pulling my memory, my experiences with all of you with me as I move on.

My hope is that my book will reach those closest to me and as many others of you as God intends.

Thank you for what I hope has been a helpful visit for you here. It's my fervent desire that CONNECTIONS moves you to know you better. Spurs you on to the growth, the realization of who you are, and embrace the God-given love that lives within you.

# ΛBOUT THE ΛUTHOR

Bob Brickley chose his "life sentence" many years ago.

*"I help people grow so they will go forth and help others grow."*

As an expert in human dynamics, he led and consulted with businesses countrywide for decades. Dedicated to the vision ... *"Growing business, by growing people."* Seven years ago, he transitioned his career to becoming a Life Coach.

Bob is a graduate of Trinity College in Connecticut. He and his wife Nancy live in Atlanta, Georgia. They have five grandchildren... including triplet nineteen-year-old boys.

Made in the USA
Coppell, TX
11 May 2023

16716729R00162